OUTCAST *With*
GOD'S
MIRACLES

JOSEPH THERANCE

Kravitz & Sons
INNOVATORS IN PUBLISHING, MARKETING AND ADVERTISING

Kravitz and Sons LLC
1301 Farmville Blvd, Suite 104
Greenville, NC 27834

Published by Kravitz and Sons LLC.

ISBN: 979-8-89639-320-7 (sc)
ISBN: 979-8-89639-319-1 (e)
ISBN: 979-8-89639-325-2 (h)

Library of Congress Control Number: 2025911130

Table of Contents

To the many people who supported my family in times of humiliation, pain, and suffering; to my grandson, Julian; and to my daughters, Tania and Jacinta, I dedicate this book.

A special thanks to my wife, Eddie Jewel Therance, my mother, Lillie B. Johnson, who supported me spiritually in time of depression. They are my Angels. Thanks to the staff at Baton Rouge General Hospital, and many other whose prayers made this possible.

I was born in America, land of the free: democratic society, vast foods, enormous wealth, land, home, a country that cares about its people and the protection of its country. But what I did not know is that there is a dark side to everything.

As the wind blew in America, on August the 24th of 1937, in the town of New Roads, Louisiana, the sun arose that morning over the banks of False River, and to the Clanton and Therance family, I was born. This was at my grandfather's home where we lived in a decent house with an indoor bathroom and galvanized roof, with four o'clock flowers along the east side of the house. I did not know what race I was, and I did not know what was to come.

My only memory of myself as a child is seeing my mother across the street at the judge's house. She was at a wash tub, scrubbing on a washboard. Incidentally, my grandfather lived in a neighborhood surrounded by people of a different color. These were very nice people. I would play and eat at their houses, and they never used the n word around me. I knew there was something different about my family, but I was too young to know exactly what it was. One day while sitting on a swing, I fell asleep while watching the tropical gardens. I fell out of the swing and was discovered in a pool of blood by a white family. This family give me medical attention.

I have a faint memory of my grandmother who, to me, looked like an Indian. She was very loveable and cared a lot about me. I remember her being sick. I was so young; I did not know what was happening. Everybody in the family was there standing outside the house. Then my grandmother asked for me, and she asked me to hold her hand and squeeze it as hard as I could. Then her strength grew weak and weaker, until there was no more strength left. Someone was crying outside, then someone took a mirror and put it to her nose and shined a flashlight into her eyes. They said she was dead. I never left her because I had so much love for her, and I did not want to lose her. Everybody was afraid of the dead and would not come into the house until the hearse from the funeral home came for her. It was a funeral home in Baton Rouge.

After her death, we moved to Baton Rouge, on Slate Street near a store. This was my first time living around blacks, and the only whites were those who lived in the store. We lived with my stepfather, who was the founder of Local 1177 Labor Union in Baton Rouge. His chauffeur was a white man. This was in 1940, so seeing a white chauffeur was rare during those times. I noticed in Baton Rouge that the city was different. The people were not as friendly as the country people I was used to being around; so, I had to make some adjustments. The blacks lived on one side of town, and whites lived on the other side. The stores and businesses were different from country stores. What I really could not understand was the water fountain separation. Why did blacks have to drink from one water fountain and whites from another one? At one refinery in Baton Rouge, there was a nice shelter for people to stand under to wait for the bus, but it was divided with a wall. The large side was for whites and the small side for colored people. On the city buses, the blacks would sit in the back, and the whites would sit in the front. I did not like this; I would always walk where I had to go. Even if it was fifteen miles, I would still walk.

The one thing to which I had a hard time adjusting was seeing how blacks were treated in stores. I remember one incident when my moth-er and I went to Tobias and Gas, a hardware store. There were a lot of white people in the store, and my mother stood there as whites continued to come in the store. The salesman, who was white, continued to ignore my mother while he waited on the whites. I got mad! I told the white salesman that my mother's money was just as good as the rest, and it was not fair that he continued to wait on the whites and not my mother. My mother told me to be quiet. That was my first encounter with prejudice. I found out quickly that the people in the city were very different from people in the country. People in the city were more open with their prejudice.

I had a lot of adjustments to make. One was at home. My stepfather had strict rules that I had to follow. First, he did not allow me to leave our yard, play with other black kids, or have visitors. The only place he would let me go to was the garden, which was about three blocks away. I had to work in the garden with a hoe at six years old. My teacher wanted to know why I had calluses on my hand. Not only did

I work in the garden for my stepfather, in the evening after he came home from work, I would shine his shoes. I saw this as an opportunity for making money.

My stepfather was responsible for getting laborers jobs. Sometimes he would get late calls for Solvay or some other plants. He would walk as far as seven miles to get a slip to the laborers so they could report to work the next morning. My stepfather was considered a prominent per-son in the community. Around the house, there were a lot of law books. An attorney would often call him and ask questions about different cases. I do not think he finished law school; however, he came from a family where one of his brothers was an undertaker and another was a doctor. His friends, both black and white, were ministers and other respected individuals. They were at the house all of the time.

As a child, we had no toys; I would read the Bible and pretend to be a preacher, but I did not understand the large words in the Bible. At night, the only entertainment we had was the radio. Every Friday night, we would congregate outside on the dark front porch where it was cool, and we would listen to the fights. At that time, the only recognition of blacks was the "Brown Boomer," also known as Joe Louis. It was a pleasure to drink lemonade while listening to the introductions and the fight. The broadcasts were sponsored by Gillette Blue Blade. They would play the music, "To look sharp, use Gillette Blue Blades. To be sharp..." and so on. This commercial continued throughout the fight. After that, my two brothers and I would climb into bed. I always slept on the end.

There was a situation that I did not like at a store downtown. Once in a while I would go there to get a hot dog, and I was not allowed to sit at the fountain. I never could understand that. How could these white people eat at my house, and I could eat at their house, but in public they did not allow blacks the same privileges as whites? I adjusted to this by not going back there anymore. I continued to shine shoes, and I charged fifteen to twenty cents. I started eating at grocery stores. I could get ten wagon wheel cookies for a nickel. The main attraction for the evening was going to the theater for about fifteen cents. I would get a Baby Ruth candy bar for a nickel. I would get three bars of candy and watch a movie, comedy, and news reel. For the first time, I was able to see what was happening in the world as far as the war in Japan. I did not under- stand what was going on, but at night at the city bus station sirens would go off and the whole town would have a black out. It scared me because I thought the town would be bombed.

It was not long after this that the war was over. We lived on Slate Street for about five years. My mother was a most industrious person, very crafty. She would save all the money that my stepfather would give her. She would take sacks and make beautiful dresses. From my stepfather's old suits, she would make suits for me, and the garden would sup-ply us with food. One time my stepfather got behind on the mortgage payments, and we were going to lose the house. My mother shocked my step-father, telling him she could handle it. This was the turning point in our lives. My stepfather and mother decided we needed a larger house, and we later moved to a house on North Thirty-First Street. There was one white family across the street, and the rest of the families were black.

We did not know, that we were about to face family tragedy. My stepfather got sick, and he was rushed to the hospital. He was diagnosed as having pneumonia and put under an oxygen tent. Late during the night, he felt like he was going to die, so he asked for me. Children were not allowed in the hospital, so they had to sneak me in the back way. When I got to the room, he had just died. This was a hard blow for my family, especially my mother. She did not know what she was going to do and how she was going to support the family.

The funeral was held at the church. I had never seen so many people, black and white. The grief was hard to bear. When a lady got up to sing a hymn, I broke down and cried. Here was the man who had welcomed me, fed me, and taken me everywhere. He had held my hands, a true friend and father, and he was no longer there for me. I exploded and left the church. I could not stand the sadness, seeing my mother and all those blacks and whites saying so many things about him. That truly was the saddest day of my life.

At twelve years old, I suddenly realized that I could no longer be a boy. Deprived of my childhood, I had to be a man. My two brothers left and joined the U. S. Army and the Marines. All that was left was my mother and me. She was grieving my stepfather's death deeply. I could see that I was losing my mother. She thought everything was coming against her. She was worried about the house; the roof was leaking. I heard her crying inside the house, and I went to comfort her. I suddenly had to find the magic words to spring her back to reality. God touched my heart to say to her, "Mother, don't worry; you know we are all loaned upon this earth."

She started laughing as she wiped her tears and said, "Boy, where did you get such an expression?"

I told her, "Don't worry, I will do all I can to help my family. For the first time, I realized that my boyhood was gone. No matter what, I had to be a man at twelve years old. I weighed about eighty-five pounds. I went into the garage to fix the roofing. I got some tacks, a hammer, and a two-by-four ladder. I strained to put on a side of the roof. The roofing weighed about ninety-five pounds. I took the bucket, climbed the ladder, and put the roofing on from the top of the ladder. How did I get it up there? Only the Almighty gave me the strength to put it up there! I dragged the roll of roofing to the edge, rolled too much out, and it slid right off the roof. The neighbors next door looked and laughed at me, but I did not give up because I was not a quitter. I put the roofing back on top, rolled a little roofing, and nailed it down. I did the whole roof and stopped the leakage. I realized what I had done. The next day I got the lawnmower, went into the white neighborhood, and cut four lawns. I came home with about fifteen dollars.

A week later my mother got a call that I was offered a job working at Christy's Drugstore behind the soda fountain. I had to get a blood test, so I went to the Health Unit. A few days later I got a call from a lady named Miss Madie Sibley, who told my mother to bring me back to the Health Unit; it was an emergency. When we got there Miss Sibley asked my mother if I suffered from anything. She told Miss Sibley that I only suffered from nose bleeds. She told my mother that I had a severe dis-ease and that I could go blind, be paralyzed for life, or die instantly. She told my mother that she was going to take care of me. She rushed me to Delgado Hospital, which was a subsidiary of Charity Hospital.

When I got there, the doctor explained to me that I had to have a spinal tap and that there were two things that could happen. If I moved while the spinal tap was inserted, I could be paralyzed or die instantly. So, we went through therapy for the spinal tap. That morning finally came, and I was escorted to the room where the tap was to occur. I prayed. I was scared to death. The doctor had me to bend over. I actually held my breath to keep from moving. I did not make any wrong moves, and everything went really smooth. Then everything changed. The pain was unbearable, and I was in bed with nurses standing by my bed for three days. My eyes were full of tears, and I could not focus. S

Something strange happened on the third day at ten o'clock in the morning. Everything turned into darkness, the pain stopped instantly; my body raised up and began to move at a high rate of speed, like a jet plane taking off the runway. I was in total darkness, but I could see a light, just as though I was looking down the barrel of a weapon. I knew then that I was no longer on this earth. I was truly at peace when this was happening. I could feel, see, and hear. I had complete control of my senses, and God had control of my spirit. I really did not know what was happening because it was beyond my control.

I did not realize what had occurred until thirteen years later. I was watching the Mike Douglas Show, and a guest was talking about her near-death experience. Suddenly, tears came into my eyes, and I was frozen on the sofa as I realized that this had happened to me. At that time, it was the near-death experience which helped me and put fear into me. I did not know whether the disease would again occur.

Life went on, and I was cutting grass one day when I got hungry and decided to go to Frank Saia's General Store. I had on khakis. I was soaked with sweat, and I was offered a job to work at the grocery store for $15 per week. By doing odd jobs, I sometimes made $15 a day, but I could only work a few days a week before I would run out of customers.

Every morning, I went to the store at 5:30 A.M., and I would sweep the front of the building, put out the display, and pump gas, all before 7:00 A.M. Then I had to go home and get ready for school. The death of my stepfather really matured me. Mr. Frank Saia, who would always talk to me and tell me things that would help me in life, also helped me to mature. He would tell me about real estate, how to work, how to save money, and how to buy certain groceries that would help my family. One of the main concerns of Mr. Saia's, was to save my soul. He would always talk to me about Catholicism, and I had a high admiration for religion.

I continued to work at the store in the morning, and after school I would work from 4:00 PM. to 6:00 P.M. When I went home, I did my homework and prepared for the next day. There was only one incident that reminded me who I was and what my place in this world was. It concerned a white lady, about twenty years old, who would stand out while I was cleaning up and had asked me if it was all right if she stood by me, because she was afraid at the bus stop across the street. Especially that early in the morning, men in cars would try to pick her up. We got to be really good friends. One morning, the milk man and the bread man were ganging up against me. The bread and milk men were talking about hurting me because of this woman. I told her, but she wouldn't stop seeing me. She called me outside the store, introduced me to her brother, and invited me to come to her home. I was afraid of what would happen to me, and I thought I would lose my job. Eventually, she left the city and returned to Mississippi, and I was able to keep my job at the store.

My schooling in the city was also a little different. I found that the teachers and students treated me as if I was a foreigner. The girls would not have anything to do with me for two reasons: I was little, and I had a light complexion. I was not accepted by girls or boys. They did have a reason not to accept me, but it was the wrong reason. During this time, the Frenchmen across town were trying to get Lincoln Theater to reserve the upstairs part of the theater for only the Frenchmen. Because of this, there was a lot of hostility, anger, and rejection. I was not accept-ed by my peer group. I remember how I would hang around the guys and try to be a part of them. A dark-skinned student struck me in my mouth with his fist, and then I knew that I would not force myself where I was not wanted.

All the way through school, I would isolate myself from other guys and girls. I learned something there. You have to accept prejudice from both sides and live with it. I have always felt that the world is large enough that there is a place for everyone. During recess I stayed in the classroom to work on my projects and study and I began to make good grades. For the first time I discovered I could make even better grades, and I was only a few points from making the honor roll.

I worked at Mr. Saia's store until I graduated from high school. One day a man was playing the slot machine in the store. He asked me how much did I make in a week. I told him twenty-five dollars per week, and he told me he could raise my salary if I would come to work for him. I began working for him, and he paid me eighty-five dollars a week on a part-time basis and on some weekends.

I walked seven miles a day, and I also enrolled in college. I went to school during the day and worked at night. There were nights I would not go to bed because I studied all night. I worked at the Baton Rouge Lithographic Company for one year. After that year I trained myself to operate the camera.

One day I walked into the publisher's office. He was in great despair. He had his head on the desk, and he was in tears. The cameraman had been killed in an automobile accident. He said, "I don't know how I am going to shoot the paper."

I said, "I will operate the camera for you."

He asked, "Can you operate the camera?"

"Yes, I said.

"Can you shoot halftones?"

Again, I said, "Yes." Halftones are the pictures reduced for columns in the newspaper. I shot everything. At the end of the week, he called me into his office and offered me a job for one hundred and twenty-five dol-lars a week as long as I put my forty hours in, even while I was a student.

I went home very happy. I told my mother that all I needed now was transportation. I finally found the car I needed, but there were two problems: I did not have all the money I needed, and I did not have a cosigner. The Trahan family was very close to me. They came to my aid whenever I had any problems. They were my mother, my father, and my brother. When I was down, they picked me up; when I was sad, they cheered me on. When I was hungry, they fed me. When I went to them and told them about the good job and told them how much the car cost, Mrs. Trahan went into another room and told her husband. They came out and gave me the money, and Mr. Trahan offered to cosign for me! This shocked me and was the starting point of my life.

We bought a 1940 Ford, and it was like new to me. I would shine the running board with shoe polish and would not allow anyone to step on the board. While working my way through college, I had no social life and no girlfriend. The girls wanted fraternity guys or football players, so that excluded me. I was afraid of having a girlfriend anyway. My near-death experience had really put fear in my heart-fear of anything and everything.

I concentrated mostly on my career and working my way through college. Then I met a friend who shared the same interests with me. We both were members of General Motors Body Craftsman Guild. His name was Alton Johnson, and we both liked sports cars. We were both design-ng cars, so he introduced me to a product called fiber glass. He built a mold and a car. I got interested in fiber glass and cars after I got too old for the guild. I missed out on the gigantic opportunity of a lifetime. I had talked a white friend of mine into joining the guild, and he and I both had invitations to the Roosevelt Hotel in New Orleans. I called to make my reservation for the workshop. The manager told me that I could not attend because I was black. My white friend got angry. When he attended, he told me what happened and said they issued scholarships. I suddenly realized that being black was a drawback, and I had to adjust to this part of the city.

Alton couldn't take being black and living in the South any longer; he went to the Art Center in California, and I continued college in the South. Before leaving for California Alton finished his fiber glass sports car. I soon began building mine. I would hang around the white shops while they were building hot cars. I was there so much, they finally invited me inside their shop. The white men were surprised to find out that I was building a car, and they came by to see it. My black neighbors were not pleased, because these men were white and they were coming to my house. I saw prejudice on both sides of the fence, from the whites and blacks. When I went to see them, however, I had no problems.

There were some prominent white men who wanted to ride in my 1940 Ford. They rode in it until a white motorcycle cop pulled us over to the side. He asked the white guys what they were doing riding in the car with a "nigger." They got angry and told him that we were looking at an engine. The police asked them if they were trying to force integration. They cleared it up, and we looked at my engine. That same cop came to the printing company where I worked several months later. My boss came into the darkroom where I was, and he asked me to come out. He had some material in his hand that he wanted me to look at and to shoot. This material was for the same cop who had called me a nigger He was now running for sheriff. When I finished his poster, you would have thought he was a black man running for office! For some reason, he lost the election!

Sometimes things that happen to you have a tendency to make you a better person in the future. I had to overcome these obstacles. I gradually began to adjust to these situations, and I did not take it as hard.

A week later, I went to a hot tamale stand. A white gentleman noticed that I had entered through the front door. He wanted to know why I did not use the back door. He was sitting in a booth in the corns and his girlfriend was sitting on the end. I told him I was a regular, and I mentioned that I had an advantage on him, standing over him. He then said he was kidding with me. By that time, the owner had come over and he put him out of the hot tamale stand.

I had to build immunities against these obstacles of life. As long as you live, you will be faced with certain prejudices brought on by folkways, mores, and traditions. Prejudice is a two-fold thing. You can acquire it from the white race and the black race. This also happened more than one time in college. The situation got so bad, I actually went home and told my mother that I could not take it any longer. I said, "I cannot make it, I cannot fight my own race. My mother wanted to know what happened, and I explained it to her. An instructor wanted me to come to her apartment to study, but I was not an idiot. I knew what she really wanted. As a consequence, she and my art instructor began plotting against me. They knew all of my business, and whatever I would tell one instructor, the other would know about it. They were conversing together and decided that they would fail me. These instructors would ask me what color my girlfriends were and in what town they lived. All of this was about light-skinned black girls and preconceived notions. I told my mother that I could not fight this prejudice, because if I did, I would not get the class card I needed for graduation. I refused to go to college that semester; I returned to work at the printing firm. I worked for approximately two months before I received a letter from the United States of America. It was a "greeting" letter to report to Fort Hood Texas, "Hell on Wheels!"

I became a squad leader, with some experience with the n-word, when one white recruit decided to test me. He was still lying in his bed when everybody else was up. When I told him to get up, he said, "Nigger, you better get out of here!" I picked him up above my head, threw him against a block wall and went after him. It took five men to hold me and calm me down. The recruit apologized; so, I did not turn him in. Eventually, this man became my best friend. The incident was forgot-ten, and after finishing basic training, I was transferred to Fort Benning, Georgia, where I worked as a specialist, lab technician, field photographer and with secret and confidential materials. I was the only black on the floor. These soldiers came from prominent families. One soldier's father was an ambassador, another had degrees from universities. I felt out of place.

A fellow from Japan, but an American, had an interest in cameras and he found out that I knew all about cameras. We became good friends and had a lot of the same interests. His name was Yoshio Marino. I had another friend from Texas named Raymond Zamora. He was Spanish and lived in Texas. One day he asked me how did I handle prejudice. I told him I experienced it on both sides and he laughed. He said, "At least you are not caught in the middle."

I asked him, "What do you mean?"

He explained that he lived on the border line between neighborhoods. On one side were blacks and on the other side were whites. He could not go the white theaters because he would get in trouble. He could not go to the black theaters either, so he had to stay at home. So, Zomora and I had something in common. Puerto Ricans and Hungarians also ran into the same dilemma. I never realized how the Puerto Ricans, Mexicans, and Blacks stuck together, until something happened. A tall, white cook also would always pick on me. If we were having pancakes, everyone would receive two, and he would give me one. If everybody got two eggs, he would give me one. One morning he caught me at the wrong time. He did it again, and I invited him outside. He said he would be there. When I got outside, there were ten Mexicans, five Puerto Ricans, and four blacks waiting. They said to me, "We are brothers, and we are here to defend you." The white cook backed down. It was said that he received so many threats that he had to be transferred.

I learned during that time that Latin Americans, Mexicans, Puerto Ricans and blacks would stick together as brothers, no matter what. I did find, however, that there is some form of prejudice in everyone. For example, there was a Puerto Rican girl who was interested in me. The Puerto Rican men called me names in Spanish which meant "dirty goat." They did this because they did not like outsiders talking to their girls. There was a Mexican girl in my department with whom I was friends, and her boyfriend was white. She came by the barracks, and we walked together to the photo lab to develop some film in the darkroom. We passed by the OCS barracks, and the troops hollered, "Nigger! Die, nigger!"

The post had a limited number of girls, and most guys were lonesome. It was off-limits for a black guy to be with a white, Mexican, or Puerto Rican girl. I remember when I was in Columbus, Georgia, looking in a showcase window at some shoes. A blond from New York start- ed talking to me and gave me her name and number. She asked me to come see her, but as the conversation was going on in the street, a cop walked up and asked her if something was wrong. She walked away suddenly, and I left. I told a Mexican friend what had happened, and he told me he knew her father. He was a colonel on the post. He said, "You don't want to date her. You will get into trouble. I left it alone.

I concentrated on my job, which was lab technician and photographer. I enjoyed my job, and I would go out and shoot landscape scenes. My best scenes were in the woods. I would set up the tripod in the center of a stream that was running water with trees in the background. As the sun would rise, the lower part of the water was darker than the upper part. Each beam of sunlight would bounce off the trees, creating a very flamboyant mood.

I had one assignment to fly to Fort Rucker, and we got there in a L-19, which was like a piper cub plane. It was nice flying above the clouds. My pilot was white, and I had no problem at all. For the first time I received a touch of freedom that I had never felt before. Being out there it didn't matter what color I was, because the attention was only on the camera. I was a private, and even generals would give me and the camera respect.

Upon returning to the post, I certainly realized that I had been somewhere some blacks had never been. I had felt what it was like to be on the other side, treated with honor and respect. I remembered what it was like to sit in the rear of the bus or go to the water fountain very thirsty and find it was for whites only. This led me to remember when I came to Columbus, Georgia. We had to ride the bus, and as we got on the only available seat was near a white lady. When I sat down, she got up, and the other white troops got angry and said nasty things to her. What probably made them angry was knowing it was all right to get shot on the front line and fight as an American, but because of my color my rights were limited.

I often wondered about people like this. People who can love, kiss, hug, and feed a dog but are incapable of loving a dark human being. Some things make me wonder how can one have so much hate. Hate is not just in the white race. I remember being in a Catholic church in Georgia, and I would always sit in the back because when church was over, I wanted to get out of there. All the pews, however, were filled up to mine. An African came up and refused to sit with me. Instead, he stood up in the back to keep from sitting down by me. Would he have done this in his country? I don't think so. When in Rome, you do as the Romans do. He saw Americans doing this, so culturally, he felt it was better for him to survive in America by doing what is expected.

It is possible that hate is like a mental or physical disease that is inherited through the genes and chromosomes and transmitted to another person. But I feel it is not inherited; it is taught by parents: "Do not even bring one of those dark things to my house and disgrace a pure family. Sometimes I wonder whether if we were all the same color, with the same texture of hair, same color of eyes, same shape of lips, same height, would we still have the same prejudices? Probably. As long as man is on Earth, he will have some prejudice. What's wrong with man? Because of greatness, he will always be indifferent; but people have one thing they do not use enough, and that is common sense. One needs to differentiate between the good, the bad, and the ugly.

In the service, time went very fast. Before I knew it, I was being processed out with one drawback. They claimed that something had showed up in my blood. They wanted to hold me until they received records from Baton Rouge. If not, I would not be discharged. They received the records, I was treated, discharged, and returned back to Baton Rouge. I was like a horse just let out of the stall, wild and crazy. But I calmed down, got my job back, and got back into college. Things were totally different; I guess because I was more mature. The factory had changed, and I was ready for life. The Army prepares you for all the challenges of life and trains you how to deal with situations tactfully.

I also went back to work in the printing company. A few things, such as the equipment, had changed. We now had a web press and a few new employees. We all got along really well; then the company hired a press-man who was a Jew. I was in charge of the composing department. It was very hard for whites to take orders from blacks. My job was cameraman, negative maker, halftones and plate maker. The Jew started harassing me by acting as though he was in love with one of the black girls that I had dumped. The girl would kiss him, hug him, and try to make me jealous. I kept my sanity when I entered the darkroom. I would take a deep breath and release the stress. This helped me to maintain my control. Then the pressman really wanted to be in charge, but the owner continuer letting me know that I was in charge. One day we had a sixty thousand run on press, and the pressman had been out all night. He thought this would be a good time to show the boss that I did not know what I was doing. So, he purposely ran the press dry so the image would break on the plate. Then he told the owner that I was making bad plates to make the boss angry with me and to make me look inferior. This worked. The boss came and chewed me out and asked me to make another plate. I did; he watched me do it and the same thing happened once again. So, I went up to see the boss and told him what was happening, explaining to him what the press needed, which was a wash down and a change in the fountain solution. I asked him to do this just as a suggestion. He then went down, told the pressman he wanted him to wash the press down, change the fountain solution, and he would get me another plate. The press ran the complete run, and the boss saw what was happening. In the meantime, I could see the boss leaning more and more toward him, so I knew it was time for me to make a move.

A refinery was running an ad that they were hiring, so I put in an application. I took the test and later received a letter telling me I failed the test. This was my second time taking the test, and I knew I had passed it. I knew that something was wrong, so I went to a federal agency. A white gentleman came out and told me to come to his office. I explained to him what happened concerning the testing. He told me that before he could arrive at a conclusion, he had to test me, and he did. He said that there was no way that I could have failed the test. He said that I had scored very high, in the supervisor's capacity. He could not train me because I was a college graduate, but he wanted me to take the test once again, then they would investigate the results. The next month I received a letter letting me know that I was hired. When I notified my boss that I was resigning, the Jewish guy could not stand the pressure. He quit and left town. Now I was going into another range of adventure-in industrial work-something that I had never before done. My godfather, who worked in that field for thirty years, told me about all the do's and do not's, the prejudices that I would encounter, the strict family operation, and what I should and should not say. We started an apprentice program with thirty-five employees. It was tough! We studied chemistry and physics. There were five blacks in the entire group; the rest were white. When completing the orientation program, only thirteen finished the program; four blacks remained with the whites. Everything my godfather had told me I found to be true. I watched the old timers; I did what they did. The blacks were not allowed to hang around the control room. They were to stay away from the smoke bench. If it was a turnaround, we learned not to hang around where they would eat. More than that, I would not hang around to listen to their jokes about blacks or remarks about Martin Luther King. When we were put on the yard with the whites, they would take a coffee break and would never invite us because they did not want to show favoritism toward blacks. This would make it bad for them. Some old timer blacks were fair, but some were not too friendly. I worked with one who was worse than working with whites. He thought he was really clever. He did everything to make me quit. He would overload the tool bag and have me carry tools we did not need to tire me out, or we would climb a two-hundred-foot-high tower. He always made me climb down eight times in one day to try to break me, but he did not realize I was already tough. Having just got-ten out of the army, my muscles were tight. We used to run twenty-four laps in the evening, and I was ready for anything.

One thing I could not adjust to was how certain family names got promotions. When blacks got a promotion, they would work twice as hard. They would work three units, and the whites would only get one unit. This was a way to break the blacks mentally. Also, the white guys who worked there would do things that would make it hard for the blacks. Blacks always got the hard jobs or the units where dangerous chemicals were located. But I realized that no matter what kind of work I had, I had to be tough. After three years I finally finished the apprentice program and was assigned shift work where I would be working for the shift superintendent. This plant was as large as a city, and wherever major breakdowns were, we handled it. I worked there for approximately three years before I got married.

Everything happened very fast. We built our house in the Crestworth subdivision; there were only three places to live for blacks. I felt like life was just beginning for me. This was only a small portion of the things to come.

After we built this house, my wife worked as a nurse at a hospital. She would not stay there very long because of the biased treatment she received from the sisters. At that time, my wife was pregnant; she stopped working for a while and enjoyed the life of a housewife.

It was Halloween night when things began to happen. My wife began feeling as though her stomach was hurting. After trick-or-treating, she came home and said she felt as though she was having diarrhea. I jumped into my 1968 Tornado, drove ninety miles per hour, and ran every light. All I could think was, "What if she has the baby in the car?" I knew nothing about first aid, but I got her to the hospital on time. She started having contractions as soon as we got into the emergency room. The staff at the hospital were the best people I had ever met. They brought us champagne, and we celebrated the birth of our first child. We were a very happy family. No one could tell me that my daughter was not mine! She had all my facial resemblances.

As time went by, before we knew it, we were having another child-a daughter! I was still working at the plant, and we had just come out of the apprentice program. I would go from one turnaround to another. Most of the time I would get the dog shift, working as a pipe fitter. It was not easy because I received prejudice from both whites and blacks. The whites would take breaks while we were working and would not tell me, because they knew the white process hands did not want me inside the control centers with them. Blacks were not allowed to eat at the tables, but they could eat in the bathrooms on a hot day. Most of the time, we would eat on the units. Some of the black mechanics would also show some prejudice, because they felt as though we were stealing their jobs; another reason was that they just did not want to be friendly.

Working in industrial plants, you have to make adjustments to all types of situations. You listen to dirty racial jokes and read racial literature. One time, I found a card from the KKK. It said that Martin Luther King and blacks stuck together and supported him-Support the Klan. During this time, it was normal to see white employees with their rebel flags on their hats and t-shirts. Some put the rebel flag on tool boxes and tool bags. Nothing was said until one employee put a black flag on his hat. The company then came up with a policy that they did not want anything on hats, tool bags, or tool boxes, nothing that would infringe upon the rights of others. This was the first time the company showed concern about employees. Actually, they did not want any confrontations that would hinder their production. These things never bothered me, because the army taught me how to deal with tense situations or stress. You have to recognize that prejudice comes from within. If you look for it, you will find it. I do not look for it and never have pre- conceived notions about a situation or person. No matter how much racism I faced, I pretended it was not there and overlooked the situation. If one looks for happiness, he will find it no matter what the situation.

I recall one day I worked in 96-degree weather, with a rain suit on, in a hole with acid fumes, with a face shield, no wind blowing, no air conditioning, and it felt like it was 114 degrees. A white friend asked me how I could smile working under such bad conditions. On a hot day I would always imagine that I was in a freezer with a big bowl of ice cream; that's why I could smile.

The situation of time affects all people. This depends on the type of people, their religious beliefs, political party affiliations, and other pressures. The Martin Luther King era, the Kennedy assassination-these situations affected our job environment; but one person who played a vital role in my life was Adam Clayton Powell. His famous expression was "Keep the faith!" No matter what happens remember no matter how hellish it seems, you can overcome all obstacles. People complain about the weather, but we cannot change the weather. Some people are not normally exposed to certain environmental conditions; so when exposed to those situations, they obviously act strange. They do not know how to respond, so they will display some ignorance. You can recognize Christians by their smile, their friendliness, their courtesy, and how they seem to be the same all of the time.

I recall one day being in the hospital, standing and waiting for an elevator; two white girls walked up. I was on the fourth floor. They refused to get on the elevator because they were afraid. The elevator went to the fifth floor, and a white gentleman got on; then it went back down to the fourth floor. When the door opened to the fourth floor, again they looked at me in shock because they would ride up with me any-way. But sometimes you have to look at the time of the incident. If a terrible crime has been committed, it could change one's personality and make him/her become more alert. We all have some tendency to hold back a little.

I recall when the incident happened in Mississippi with Tillman and Meger Evers, the atmosphere and personalities of the people around me at work changed. Nothing was said, but when the incident with O. J. Simpson happened, you could feel and hear the surrounding atmosphere. News media had quadruple coverage the papers ran away with it. Everywhere you went you could hear white people talking about it, and I could feel how much prejudice still existed in America. Did you think the same feeling existed for Martin Luther King's assassination as when the Goldman family asked for O. J. to pay damages for the death of Ron?

There is something wrong in America; race relations are in bad shape and need to be reconstructed. Racism is taught, not inherited. If we could pray and accept one for who he or she is and not what his or her color is, we would have one of the most productive countries in the world, I think as long as we live there will be some prejudice. If I were in a world where all people looked alike and had the same color and same texture of hair, there would be indifference; some people thrive upon their prejudice, so personalities would be different. We have to over-come our dilemma and prejudice; we need no hate, but healing.

Sometimes we fail because of our family; they do not teach us properly. I always make a point to be friendly to everyone and to break the barrier first, even if I am insulted. That way you at least know where you stand and know how to deal with it. When you are in a certain environment, you can anticipate certain things. If you are in a night club, you can expect something to happen, especially in a highly tense area.

Working in an industrial area, there were situations when certain engineers came around the units, and especially around black mechanics, they would refuse to shake hands. I remember when an engineer, fresh out of college, came on the units, and he shook hands with all of the black mechanics. It was not long before they called him into the front office. The next time he came out, he was another person. I told the black mechanics that it would not take long before he learned how things operated around here.

The shift superintendent had an emergency on one unit, so the mechanics rushed over there, blissed the job, and gave it to process to run a test to be sure there were no leaks. All the mechanics then went to take a break. We were all sitting on the smoke bench, and an engineer just hired, whom the company had brainwashed to be hard on mechanics, saw the mechanics on the bench. He came over and wanted to know our names, and we gave them to him. He went into the control room, called the superintendent, and reported that he found three black mechanics loafing on the smoke bench. The only problem was that he reported three blacks, but there were only two blacks and one Italian.

The Italian got really upset and demanded an apology. He mentioned that the man was wrong two ways. One, we were not loafing; we had just blissed the job so the unit could get back into service. Two, he had his people mixed up. The engineer only did what the company told him to do. This was a strategy maneuver of mechanic engineers.

People who were in authority did not want to comply with federal regulations, and they had their own means of promotion. I once talked to a white co-worker who, because of his name, knew he would move to a top position because a family member was his sponsor. Whites could take advantage of promotions when there was a job or position open. The only time the blacks would hear about it was after it was announced in a newsletter. By that time, it was too late to apply. Information can be segregated to deny people their rights. In the company telephone directory, one could see how the company operated as a family. This is one reason why certain blacks and whites did not get hired; they did not have a sponsor from their family.

I trained new employees who told me they would be my supervisor as soon as they got out of the apprentice program. Even though I had experience, I was not part of the immediate family. At private dinners, country club meetings, and family reunions, it was impossible for me to be there when job openings were being discussed. Being black, there were many gates to success closed to me.

Sometimes when gates are closed you have to reset your goals, as when you go hunting deer. If you miss your deer, you do not pick up your gear and go home. You reset your sight and wait for another opportunity. Being black, I think positive, even when negative forces come against me.

After working shifts for more than eleven years, one shift was taken off because the plant was downsizing, and I was put back on day shift. In this way I had larger exposure to new conditions. The supervisor assigned me to a mechanic when was a former boxer. He was a nice white gentleman who was a lot of fun. One morning I spoke to him, and he walked out on the unit and did not respond to me. Later he came back and apologized to me. He told me that his wife was dying of cancer and he needed to be by himself, but I could not do that. I talked to him and kept his mind occupied; before you knew it, I had him laughing. Sometimes, you have to forget about how people treat you when they are troubled and do God's work.

He informed me about policy and how to get along with process personnel. First, do not sit in the control room or be caught eating in the control room. One thing I noticed, whenever there was a big nasty job, I could expect to be working that area. This was noticed on most units where blacks were working. To keep a positive attitude, you have to build a block wall in front of you and allow no one to penetrate your wall with negative forces, no matter what happens. After working on the unit for three years, the unit consolidated, which required more work and new assignments.

By this time, the federal government had forced industrial plants to hire more women. The white plant workers could adjust to some white women being hired, but they could not adjust to the black women. In one unit, I had to call a process operator outside and threaten to go before his boss and file a complaint. I asked, if that was his wife or moth-er, would he want other men to disrespect her and suddenly he realized what I was saying. He apologized, but months later he could not stand it, so he resigned.

Another incident involved a black woman who had a miscarriage while working. The area plant managers knew about it, so they just looked over it; but the lady could have had a big law suit. She decided to let it go. There were a lot of incidents that went unreported, and they just let them get away with it, because they feared that their jobs would be in jeopardy. Another black lady was called into the office to talk with the supervisor. She was told that if she wanted a promotion, she had to follow their rules; To move right to the top would require a little hanky-panky. This occurred on many jobs and still happens today, and it has been happening ever since slavery. It is happening today, but they are more open with it.

After changing to the day shift, I was assigned to work at a building that made rubber. The majority of the men working there were black. The temperature got to 114 degrees during the day, and at night it was still hot in the building. Most blacks caught hell in that building. I remembered when we had tremendous rain for a long period of time. That morning, I got up and looked outside to see how much water was in the street. It was about 5:00 A.M., and I wanted to see if the streets were flooded, and they were. I thought I saw someone's garbage bag floating in the street, so I went and made some coffee to clear my head and wake myself up. After drinking the coffee, I looked outside once again, and when I did, I realized that it was an alligator. I walked down the carport and saw a sheriff with a rifle by his side. He told me to get inside, and I was not allowed to move my car. So, I called in and told my supervisor I would be late.

The wild life people came and agitated the alligator. He ran under the neighbor's car, took his tail, and lifted up the car. They allowed some time to pass, then placed a towel upon the alligator's face. The alligator got really quiet, they placed a wire loop on his tail, pulled the wire loops together, and tied them. It took five men to lift him and place him into a wooden crate.

It was time for me to go to work, and I needed a late slip. Here I was, a black guy, having to tell the guards I was late because an alligator was in my driveway. One of the guards looked at the other guard and asked me what did I want him to write on the slip to the supervisor. I told him to write that an alligator was in my driveway, and they wrote that on my slip. When I got inside the finishing building and gave the slip to my supervisor, he was talking to another process operator supervisor. The mechanical supervisor looked at the late slip, laughed, and said, "What an excuse!" The next day, the newspaper covered the story. It was placed on the bulletin board: "Ten-foot alligator found in Crestworth Subdivision, weighed over three hundred pounds. Then the guards believed me.

As time went on, there were changes brought on by the government. New employee adjustments had to be made, and the company was fighting the union policies. In the meantime, contractors began to invade the company. New company policies were being enforced. Before we knew it, contract employees were everywhere, and the company was no longer hiring any more mechanics. While black employees were advancing into mechanical jobs, all white mechanics were forced into a supervisor's program. We were right back where we had started before the orders had come to headquarters from the federal government. When they got through with it, their relatives still wound up with the positions. This policy will continue until the companies change. After all the years of the federal government enforcing the discrimination policy, the major corporations had shifted to another policy and hired relatives anyway. If you wanted to see the percentages, all you needed to do was stand by the parking lots, and you would see how many blacks were working in industrial plants and how many whites were working there.

Because of this situation, I felt my job would be in jeopardy; I also decided I needed to have something to do when I retired. I opened a grocery store which my wife ran. We were doing really well, and it was an established business. It was owned by an Italian family for more than one hundred years. The area population consisted of one-half blacks and one-half whites. I knew what I was up against and anticipated some rejection by the white race. A small number of whites continued to patronize our store, and there were many white families who would not accept a black man in business. I ignored those who would not accept me. One problem was the building inspectors who were really nasty. They wanted me to add more sinks in the meat department. It was all right for the white owners, but the inspector wanted to give me a hard time.

After about a year of running the business, we heard we were going to have a robbery; undercover cops staked out the warehouse. The robbery did not materialize. I told my wife to open the store in front, but for some reason, she parked in the rear. My sister-in-law could not open with her, so she sent her son to open with my wife. The robbery happened that morning. The young man was wearing a ski mask, armed with a butcher knife. My wife saw that he was running toward her with the knife drawn like he was going to stab her; so my wife told her nephew to shoot the gun. He fired a shot, but the robber continued coming toward her and tried to stabbed her. At the same time, he tried to grab the money sack. My nephew fired another shot, and the bullet hit the wall of the wall cooler and glazed off the wall, just missing her head.

This all happened early in the morning while it was dark, which made it difficult for them to see anyone. After the bullet grazed off the coolers' wall, my wife went inside the store, called the sheriff, and reported the robbery. As daybreak came, they noticed a body laying in the alley way. A man was shot, so they rushed him to the hospital and pronounced him dead.

I was at work when I received an emergency call telling me to report to the store. Upon arriving at the store, there were light gray vehicles all around the parking lot. When I got inside, the investigator was questioning my wife; I asked my employee, Leonard, what had happened. He told me there was a robbery and someone was killed, so the detective asked me to close the store because they feared revenge by the dead man's family. I remained open, but the customers refused to come, so we closed.

Business gradually increased, but the atmosphere was never the same. The fear was always there. This incident destroyed my wife, and it destroyed friendships. I could see in later years how drugs were infiltrating that area. There were young men who would stand on the corner selling drugs. I could see the business was decreasing because of the drug activity in the area. We noticed more crime was occurring and more break-ins. Some nights, I would get a call that my alarm was on; I would rush to the store immediately. I had to drive about seven miles, and I would get there and find someone had burst a hole in the wall. Another time, they had broken into the Coke machine. Times were very hard because this business relied upon farmers, laborers, plant workers, and families. The drugs in the area cut a big hole into my profits.

I had to make some adjustments. When you cut back on profits and products, it really hurts your business. Times were inflationary, and the government was trying to make adjustments that were not working. I borrowed money to try to restock my business, which helped the business get going again; but business has it's cycles, sometimes good and sometimes bad.

The bread man walked into the store and would never speak. I immediately suspected something was wrong with him or the situation;

I began to watch him. I knew something was wrong, and I was right. I noticed the color code for each day was a different color, so I called the supervisor. He asked me what were the colors, but before I could tell him, he told me he was coming down. When he got there, he noticed the bread was stale. He immediately got angry and told me he was going to fire the man. I asked him not to because he had a family; but I did ask him to take him off our route. This was something I did not need, but prejudice comes from many angles when you are down.

I have never been able to understand how the government operates, why it treats people so inhumanely in a democratic society. Is it the government, or is it the people empowering themselves to do what they want because they are sadists? In our government, we allow the tax system to operate as a separate entity. The only thing the Internal Revenue Service cannot stop is auditors from allowing their prejudice and pre-conceived notions to get into their work. The citizen's family gets hurt if they get involved.

A white friend going into an office with a white auditor has a better advantage than a black guy walking into Internal Revenue as a black citizen. The business was doing well, then a black man came in, looked around, did his survey, and acted really okay, but he had to do what the whites told him to do. Like I told you, there are things that happened to me that, being a non-biased person, I thought would never happen to me because I was brought up in a white neighborhood, in a small town where I did not know about prejudice.

When I opened a store, however, the odds were against me. I had forgotten I was still living in the South. The pressure would be coming our way from all directions; I had to continue fighting all obstacles with an iron fist. But no matter what you believe, how do you fight the system of the United States?

As months went on, I thought I had a chance living in the system; but no matter what happens, the odds are against you. As my grocery business began to progress, another obstacle hit us very hard. The auditor from Internal Revenue called and told my wife that they were doing a general survey, so we would need certain papers showing our invoices and tax papers. We were prepared; however, we did not expect what was to come. The lady from Internal Revenue was very nasty. The way she acted, you would have thought that she was God. Before my wife spoke, I informed her to be nice to the lady, to offer her coffee. But this was one biased lady, and she first acted as though the office was not clean enough for her. When my wife called and told me she was white and that she was very nasty, I knew the odds were against us.

The auditor called daily asking for certain papers, and she continued to call repeatedly. Upon coming home from the store in the evening, my wife would be in the bathroom vomiting. The constant harassment caused her to get sick, so I told her I would be bear all responsibilities in dealing with the Internal Revenue. The I.R.S. works like the army; the auditors get their orders, and they do anything to carry out their orders. There is a strategy behind everything they do. Later, we received letters from the IRS telling me of an interview. My wife and I looked up all the papers and I called my tax man and dis-cussed our strategy; but the tax man showed me where I did not owe any money. My tax man told me he wanted to be there for the interview. When we got there for the interview, I noticed that the auditor had her supervisor sit in on our interview. This told me that the auditor was new in this job, so I had to watch everything she was doing. I was alert for everything she presented.

One thing she did was tax items that had already been taxed. I explained to her that she was to separate the grocery from other items, but she had to hurry and get her papers to headquarters. I was not satisfied with the interview. There was something funny about these two white women teaming up the way they did. I had experiences as a black person dealing with white woman. They were prejudiced and when I walked into the room, I know what I was up against. One thing about being black is having the instinct of knowing what you feel inside when a situation is good and when a situation is bad. If you look at a person's eyes, this will tell you a lot about the personality of the individual. What I read in their eyes was not good. Fear, hate, anger, racism- these are the things that blacks will receive for the rest of their lives. Even God cannot help these people, because they enjoy inducing pain upon people and families. Living in America will always be this way, because the government allows this to happen. Look how long it took for the government to recognize black men equally-not until Martin Luther King.

After the interview with the Internal Revenue, I filed a complaint to the IRS's higher office. The lady came from New Orleans, and she told me she had the power in her pen; she talked honestly. We signed papers to try to relax my wife because she had a nervous stomach. We decided on a monthly payment, but when the signed papers reached the Nashville office, they changed it to what they wanted. We continued to run our business, but after this incident with the federal government, my wife was upset because we truly didn't do anything wrong. But as you discover, the government can do whatever it wants to do.

I could not believe what was happening to me, but I assume was common in the South. Several of my other black friends who were in business said this was happening to them also. It seemed like they were attacking black business. I felt my exposure to prejudices had never happened, because all the white I knew were very nice people-no problems whatsoever.

Our business started function again, and we thought we were getting back to normal. Then we received a letter from a federal judge ordering the store closed. We decided to file for bankruptcy and tried to save our home, but the Internal Revenue would not leave us alone. They stopped my family from functioning, because most of our money had to go to the I.R.S. I wonder if when the I.R.S. first started, was it more likely to aid the people? Now the I.R.S. is more like an enemy of the people. I often wonder what it would be like to live in this country without the fear of doing something wrong.

Being audited again really did something to my wife's health. She continued getting sick, so we decided to take her to the doctor. They dis-covered that she had Lupus. This was not good; she was rushed to the hospital. She could not hold any food into her stomach and was dehydrated. She stayed about a week and was later discharged.

After another week, she got sick and dehydrated again; this time she lost a lot of time, and we were getting behind on the bills once again. My wife looked as though she was not getting any better, and because we were so far behind in our bills, we decided I should retire from the plant.

The separation took a couple of months; so I continued to work to help pay some of the bills. After working in the plant for more than twenty-five years and being exposed to all types of situations, it was not hard to leave. I had seen explosions, fires, and many other crises, almost got burned twice, a probe blew out near me, and had a hand picked up by a crane. Why my hand did not break, I do not know, except that God was protecting me. Another incident occurred when I was first hired. The units had compressor houses, and one morning-coming into the plant halfway asleep-when walking through the compressor house, I found out that the odor of ammonia will wake you up.

Since I was retiring from an industrial plant with more than three thousand five hundred employees, a retirement party was given. Everyone came to wish me well, and the most emotional part of the situation was watching my supervisor cry. We had a good bond. He shared all my troubles: seeing my wife weak, understanding what I was facing, relating to my wife's illness and the many bad things that continued to happen to me and my wife's family-like bad luck was hanging over us, like something created by Hollywood or a man-made story.

After retiring, I spent a lot of time cooking, cleaning the house, and taking care of my wife. I enjoyed doing this, especially for my wife, but I had to condition myself for the stress of sickness, the I.R.S., and other obstacles that kept appearing in my life. The army had physically conditioned me to deal with the stress. The only problem was trying to understand why these things were inflicted upon my family. I could not find out why God let these things happen to me. I guess I was a victim, not of circumstance, but of the way man constructed society, the way he could make money. The laws that are enforced by the I.R.S. do not affect them; the system was designed for poor people, which is wrong. We are citizens of the United States. I know for sure that the Internal Revenue Service interfered with my Bill of Rights, and that is the freedom of religion, the right to own a home. What happened to Internal Revenue is it is getting out of hand. Any time in America when a branch is operating in the government as separate entity, then it is time that we revise our system: its law, interest procedure, strategy, collection policies, and requirements. Auditors should need to get degrees, and in the curriculum, they should be taught the psychology of dealing with people-how to talk to people.

Internal Revenue needs to condense its laws so it, too, can understand. I recall one time when my attorney was connected on a three-way call, the auditor was on the line telling me what I could not do. What she didn't know was that my lawyer was on the other line. My lawyer cut in because she was advising me incorrectly. He told her she could not do this, and she told him he didn't know what he was talking about. She went on explaining it, and finally, when my attorney advised her that he was an attorney, she rephrased what she was saying and she would not talk anymore. She knew that she was not as up to par as she should be.

I never realized how the Internal Revenue would interfere with my religion until-after being honest all my life and believing in people, especially people serving the public-I saw that they would do injustice against me, especially the lady who audited me. How do I know for sure that she did my taxes without considering ethnic backgrounds and pre-conceived notions? She smiled and acted very friendly, went and got coffee for me, and screwed my eyeballs out on paper. You cannot pay attention to the auditors. The auditors in the office cannot be trusted. They should be there to try to help the public, but somehow our tax department has gotten out of control. You see it happening on the news. Actually, what the I.R.S. did to my family created welfare. They caused my family to pay money we did not owe. The government was com-mitting a crime against families, taking food from their mouths. So when they go to get food stamps, the government is not defeating their purpose. When Internal Revenue handicaps a family, it causes sickness, worry, and death. Should American democracy have to put up with this?

Are our tax laws invading the Bill of Rights of citizens? Each time we were audited and not treated properly, it had an effect on my wife. She was actually scared of the I.R.S. She had a nervous stomach, and soon her food would not stay in her stomach. She continued to vomit, and she was put back into the hospital. It had developed into Lupus by this time. She began to do better, but the steroids seemed to take a strange effect on her, causing more vomiting again. After being home for no more than a day, she had to be rushed back to the hospital. This time, after being in bed so long, she lost the use of her legs. The letters steadily came in from the I.R.S., asking for money that was not there, probably quadrupling in interest. This reminded me of crawfish in a bucket-once you get down, you will never get back on your feet.

It created a tremendous dilemma. I had to eat one meal a day so my family could survive. I had paid more than thirty thousand dollars-this was the money for intended food, shelter, medicine, and tuition. As you know, when one problem is created it causes another problem. This tells me there is something wrong with the system. You see it every day on the streets with the homeless. Our American politicians are ignoring the main problems that the system is causing for American families. Is our tax law too rigid? Is it fair to families on limited income? Is there too much interest? Is it respecting families? Should our government operate like a Gestapo? When taxes cause a family to lose everything they have-including their home-then we are stealing from our American families.

Every time I see a hurricane clean out houses in a neighborhood or a tornado wipe out homes in Texas, I sympathize with families, because after serving in the army for this country and paying taxes for more than fifty years, when I retired all the money accumulated for retirement was again re-taxed. Are we overtaxing our citizens? After fifty years of paying taxes, we get these thanks from our government. They thank us by kicking us in the gluteus maximum. It seems that today, while we are kicking American families out of their homes for taxes, they will move some of the foreigners into our place. Is this the American way? The system needs to be revised. When one law interferes with another law, then something is wrong and is not balancing. The I.R.S. interfered with my Bill of Rights. When all these things were happening to my wife, I could not face God. I would choke up in church and start thinking about how evil people are. How can they do these things that they do and go home and act as though nothing happened?

There were times I could not see the value of life. There were times I really wanted to commit suicide, because more and more, I could see that life in America has no value. It seemed like when I went to church, the mass would always relate to what was happening to my family. When I would hear it, I would choke up and tears would pour down my face. I would walk out of church; I could not stand it. It would remind me of the day I went to a funeral, so I would leave. When I was working at a plant, to keep myself from being seen I would hide behind the control board. As you can see, it not only interfered with my religion, it interrupted my everyday life. I had to keep everything together and not let my family fall apart. I had to condition my mind by thinking constructively. But most of the time, when things get so bad, you can pray and pray, and there is no other place to go but to God. That is the only friend. I went on with life, but as you know, the problem will never go away. Probably the only thing that will separate man from all the evil is death. This part, the Internal Revenue has no power over, and that is death-only God has that power.

Finally, my wife got better, so I decided to go to check on my moth-er. While riding, something told me to go to my mother and check on her. So, I drove straight over there and found a fire truck and an ambulance in front of her house. I went inside and saw her on the floor. They were giving her oxygen. One of her tenants had called E.M.S. and she was rushed to the hospital. She was treated and released. Then one day Mother told me she had not heard from her son in a long time, so she wanted me to drive her to his apartment. When we got there and he finally opened the door, he really looked awful. He could hardly catch his breath. Mother thought he had AIDS. I decided we should call E.M.S. Upon their arrival, they thought he had pneumonia. They put him on oxygen, walked him down the stairs and rushed him to the hospital. There they discovered that he had a collapsed lung. After this, they put him into a nursing home.

One day while home, I got a call telling me that my brother had died and I needed to get over there. When I got there, the nurse escorted me to my brother. He died with a smile on his face. I had talked to him before he died, and he was very happy. He had straightened himself with God, and he told me he was ready and very happy. I went home to tell my mother that her son had just died. I was really afraid to tell her. How do you tell an eighty-three-year-old that her son has died? I hurried to get away from the nursing home and tell her. As we walked outside, my wife noticed my mother driving her car around the corner. As she pulled up and shut off the engine, she could see in my eyes that something was wrong. She asked me what had happened, and I asked her to get out of the car and have a seat in the back of the car. Then we took her to the room. She was very satisfied to see him with a smile on his face. It was as though he was telling us everything was all right.

I buried my brother; that was some stress relieved from me. Although my wife was still ill, we were able to make it through. After burying my brother, I went home and looked into my mailbox, and there were more letters from the I.R.S. and United Companies, letting me know that I had just lost my house. Internal Revenue sent me a nice letter to let me know they were going to put a lien on the property that I did not own. What a nice way to spend the day after attending your brother's funeral! Wouldn't it be really nice to wake up one morning and find that you did not have to pay any taxes? That you no longer have to live in fear that someone would knock down your door or do something to your family? As long as you have life in your body, you will live in fear. I know I will never catch up in my taxes because of the cost of living, and when you do not have the money, the interest continues to build up as the years pass. You never catch up. Interest continues, and never will you be relieved until you die.

One auditor told me, "You can compromise, but this is only for the wealthy, because they are the only ones who have the money to com-promise. Little people do not have money to compromise; so this opportunity is only for the rich."

After my brother's death, my wife and I moved into an apartment, because the house we built-our dream home had been lost because of the I.R.S. They told us we had so much to pay, and this crippled our finances, causing the lack of the funds that would normally pay for our home. This hurt me badly, and my wife and kids took it really hard. I could not tell my mother, because I was afraid it would cause her to have a heart attack. She did not find out until later. Believe me, it was an embarrassment for me, too. But, as you know, I was not in control of my destiny. My life was being controlled by the United States Government. The government in the democratic society in which we live. This is the American way! I used to hear Don King say, "Only in America!" I didn't know what he meant, but now I understand.

After moving into the apartment, I had to adjust to a new way of life. Everybody was all cramped into one small area. Noise had become a fac-tor. I was not getting enough sleep; some of these people in the building never went to bed. The I.R.S. was still calling me about making payments.

Finally, one good break! My wife was offered a new job, and she would be working for a nursing home; however, she was fired later. She was offered a new job making about twenty dollars an hour. I was thinking that this was my opportunity to get back into business. My wife was doing really well, and we were about to buy a new home. But something told me this would not last very long. As we began to make money again, we got a call from the I.R.S. that they were going to put a lien against my property, and we would have to pay two hundred dollars a month. My wife started paying taxes, and before you knew it, she had gotten sick again, and we had to rush her back to the hospital. She was walking perfectly, and one evening I heard something rumble in the kitchen. My daughter and her fiancée picked up my wife who had fallen on the floor. Her legs had given out on her, causing her to fall. The next morning, she got up out of her bed and fell to the floor once again. She called the doctor, and they told her to go back to the hospital. They proceeded to give her medication for two days. They did a M.R.I., which found that the Lupus had caused a stroke on her spine. She took the bad news in good faith.

She explained to me the danger of Lupus, how the tissue could move to an area that could cause her instant death. The first time the tissue had moved to the brain, causing her to have three seizures, and with treatment the tissue was removed from the brain. This allowed for her to get better, but then it moved to the spine. After all this, she still had a positive attitude. Being a nurse, she had a good understanding of what to expect in her condition.

America, in the 1940s and '50s brought about gradual changes, even though the races were separated in both housing and commercial aspects. The '60s saw another era. In my environment we still had black families that were on one side of town, and whites were on another side. With the assassination of President Kennedy, I could see something happening to our government that was very dissatisfying. Within the political parties, spying was revealed. Watergate revealed what was actually happening all the time, except this time they got caught. The changes were being seen in the workplace. For the first time, blacks became the center of attention. Rebellion by white pressure groups became more evident.

Race relations began to show signs of improvements. In some areas of the South, there were some rejections, but Louisiana made tremendous improvements. Some whites in Baton Rouge, however, all of a sudden had real estate sign popping up everywhere. Walker, Prairieville, Gonzales, and Hammond saw a tremendous growth. Some families did not want to integrate, so they moved to keep their kids from being around blacks. As hard as the Federal government tried to enforce the law, the people were going to do whatever they wanted to do. As the government tried to enforce integration, the people diverted to another plan. One never knows what an individual goes through unless he or she walks in the other's shoes.

Being in the hospital with my wife all the time, I saw what pain and suffering is like. When there is too much pain, there is a tendency to do something negative. In all that one has to go through to live and survive, the odds of enjoying life are impossible. We are still not as bad as other states, however, that have had incidents that are embarrassing to the entire country.

When my wife was in the hospital, we found the whites very open-hearted. Everyone there was working together, and they were like angels of God. They really took my heart.

Since the '60s, I have found that after the assassination of Kennedy and Martin Luther King, the south has made more improvements than any region, especially in the workforce and in public places.

What I am talking about are people who are racists but do a good job of hiding it, no matter what job they have, whether a doctor or nurse. When I was a little boy, where I was born, I did not experience racism in that small, country town. But when I came to the city, it was obvious what was going on. In the '40s and '50s, racism was more prevalent. They did not camouflage themselves. They were open in response to action. When you went in a store in Baton Rouge, the whites were always waited on first, or the salesman would ignore you as though you were not there. You would have to wait until all the whites were waited on. In the '40s and '50s, the schools were segregated. The whites lived on one side of town, and the blacks lived on the other side of town. Blacks were not allowed to go to the white schools, universities, or trade schools-every source of education was denied.

It was known in the workplace that blacks could only mingle with whites in the workplace. At dinner time, blacks ate only with blacks, and whites ate with whites. I, myself, never could understand these actions of American culture, but in a sense the government catered to this perception and American custom.

I could never understand how black women who were nannies took care of white children, and when they saw them in public, they acted as though they did not know them. I remembered when I was a little boy hearing my boss talk about a governor who once said, you have white men who have their white women during the day, and at night they are with their nigger women. They wanted to say the governor was crazy, but his wife said he was only speaking the truth. The white public did not want to hear the truth. I have worked around white people who joke with me around the workplace, but when they get around the public, they act as though they did not know me. I never could understand how a nurse could take care of a white patient, and when seen in public, she acted as though she did not know the patient and family.

In the city where I live, there has been some progress as to race; but we were always integrated at night in this city. There was a part of town where whites drove through the black neighborhood all night long. It was known as Seventeenth Street. The individuals were all kind. Then there was another part of town where they would drive in the back of this house, and the white men would come there during the day. The police knew about this place, but they would not do anything about it because there were too many distinguished whites who came there.

There are a lot of whites who I know who acted like a racist during the day, but at night the tiger came out of them. White men during this time dominated everything. It was the white men that gave black women babies, but they got away with it because of who they were. I know of black girls who look white and have white families. I know of one used car salesman whose daughter is black, and the girl looks identical to him and has all of his features. There is one thing that I can say, the white women had more pride as to going with black men; but then again, the white men had complete control of their white women, even though the white men did exactly what they wanted. Even today, the pride of white women is the same; however, some white women have become more open to black men. I remember a white woman said her husband was beat up and robbed. She made it appear as though her husband was doing the right thing. Undoubtedly, she was brainwashed by him, or she was ignorant to the facts and knew nothing about the area where he was. That particular area was always infested with prostitutes at night. It was a black area. Why was he riding in the black area? It was only with one purpose and that was to let the tiger out of him. He definitely was looking for something at midnight, and it surely was not drugs. Sometimes I will detour, because there is so much white traffic at night, you would think you were going to a football game. Some black women were fascinated with white men. I have been places where the giggle was over exaggerated or every time you saw them, they were up in their faces.

I remember going to a department store, and a black sales lady saw me when I walked into the store. She was talking to a white friend, total-ly ignored me, and acted as though I did not exist. There was a black woman who actually looked as though she was white and wanted the government to change her birth certificate to say she was white.

Our government has difficulties with racism because, for a long time, they would not enforce the laws, and they allowed things to happen. For example, I used to think that as Americans we are free, with certain rights, but they do not say that. They say we are Afro- Americans; in other words, those whites who come to this country are recognized as Americans. Is this a form of discrimination by our government? You be the judge! In Mexico, if you are a citizen of Mexico, you are called a Mexican-American. There are black Americans who feel this country needs to revise and change its political structure and its constitution, which discriminates against its people.

Even today, this country promotes racism and allows certain things to happen without doing anything about it immediately. For many, many years there was discrimination in housing, education, jobs, and many other areas. Some avenues have been opened, but then there are certain areas that are camouflaged. In certain areas when a black person calls a real estate company, they hear you are black and the house is sold. But two months later you go out there, and the house is not sold.

I often wonder what it would be like to be white for just a few months, with all the avenues open: jobs, education, and finances. It has to be a good experience in life.

No, not in God's church! All men are created equal, but then you see people leave their jobs for the weekend. Come Sunday, the whites go to their churches and receive their communion, and the blacks go to theirs. I remember, even Catholic churches yielded to what the political system allowed. At least they did allow blacks to come inside the church and did not turn them around at the front door. I cannot imagine heaven. when you get there, with all blacks on one side and whites on the other side. I realize that as long as you live, people will be indifferent, some thinking they are better than you. There are also blacks who think they are better than other blacks.

Religion is something that is very sacred. We have to give honor to God, regardless of our differences in denomination. We have to put away our prejudice and remember that God made everybody with everything the same. Even though we are not in the same church, we know deep in our hearts that people are different. It was not the intent of God to separate love, faith, and hope in man, but to unite man in a peaceful environment. The behavior of others is not the teaching of God, but the act of the devil. God, I think, would love to see man like one big family, with the same love and Christian understanding, pursuing the same goal, and preparing man for heaven.

God made religion to keep man under control and to keep unity among the races. Instead, man fixed it the way he wanted it in his environment. Why can man not accept God's children for the Spirit and not their color? What do they have to fear? Is it that they would lose their control, or do they fear this is a sign of weakness?

One of our rights is the freedom of religion. Is it honored? Can a black man go to any church he wants? The answer is no! Can the government force churches to do what it wants them to do? I do not think so. Man han to construct these churches himself.

I remember once in church; I decided to sit on a private bench. I really wanted to pray. When I got situated in church, a white woman came in and wat by me; then when she sat, looked to her side, and realized that she wan allotting next to a black man, she suddenly got up and sat in another pew. When it was time to go to communion, she was the first one up there. Did she fool God? I do not think so. To her it was all right, and she had not done anything wrong. She has been practicing this act all the time; she saw her parents do this. To her, there was not anything wrong. Then again, what would others think if they saw a white woman sitting on the same pew with a black man?

I do not think God is blind. I am very sensitive to the fact that white people move an extra pew away from blacks. This is not a good sign. They want to go to church, but they just don't want their friends to see them sitting next to a black. One time in a Catholic church, they would allow parishioners to shake hands with one another to help spread the godliness of the church. At first, they would make a point to sit next to their friends and not around a black person. I noticed this. To avoid changing my mood in church, I made it a point to always sit in a corner, off to myself, so I could remain in good faith. There is something wrong with man, when he thinks that God loves only one race, and your race is the only true race.

There are some whites who do not mind who they sit around and with whom they associate. They are identified by other whites as "nigger lovers." I once met a white gentleman in the army, and I was the first black he had ever been around. He told me he lived on a mountain that was really isolated from people, or you might say, black people. A lot of whites act the way they do because they have not been exposed to blacks before, only through preconceived notions.

Religion and society are like being in college. What the upperclassman does sets the attitudes for the entire student body. I know that in Baton Rouge there is a church where all the college students go; when I went there, some groups would still isolate themselves by sitting in a certain section, and this was going on inside the church. Some people really think they can fool God, but God is not blind.

Hate is like a disease; it is taught, not inherited. The root of hate is what is taught by family. What can I do to prevent anyone from hating me? Well, at the workplace, I would try to be extra-friendly and avoid talking about racist items; then there is no compromise. There is not an ounce of hate in my bloodstream. White Americans do not see a major problem in this country. Blacks, however, are more pessimistic about race relations. I never could understand why I do not hate anyone; I love everyone upon this earth. I have always wondered what caused one to hate. I once had a person call me a name. I got angry, but I did not hate the person, because you have to walk in someone's shoes to understand why they act the way they do. I have become accustomed to under- standing various cultures. There may be some I do not like, but I learn to honor and respect them.

One only gets one chance at this life. Every second in life is important. What you do upon this earth has a large impact upon getting to see God. I am very proud that God gave me a chance to live upon this earth as a civilized human being and not as an animal that lives in the jungle. There are, however, some who are human beings but are living like animals. With every ounce of breath that God has given me, I cherish just being upon this earth.

Personally, I have always been fascinated by other races because of their dialects, folkways and cultural histories. I am not the only one, because there are many families who take vacations to see the other people of the world and how they are living. The amazing thing about life is living, and as long as there is God and religion, people are going to have to live together. God did not want people to hate each other because of the texture of hair, the color of skin, the size of the person, or the culture of a person.

I try to look at myself and find out why a person does not like me. It could be a childish action, but most people who hate are the ones who cannot tell you why they hate. -like Hitler, who wanted a pure race with no Jewish blood and no black blood. What he really wanted was to be God. He desired the world to be the way he wanted it to be; he later found out that he had no control of his destiny. I think what causes one to dislike another, could be jealousy, because they are not as smart, or you do not do the same things they do, or you just do not have things in common. From love to hate, when two people have lived together for a long time, one morning they wake up and all of a sudden, these people cannot get along any more. When we look at someone, we try to find our values. If these values are not there, then some form of discrepancy will occur. Everybody in society wants to be identified with someone or some culture. Belonging to someone is important. Even an old stray dog wants to be identified with some culture or family, so he keeps wandering around until he finds someone that will accept him.

One thing I have learned is that everybody has a heart, but the soul is developed by family values and culture. If the soul is developed with spiritual values, then the soul will show proper values. One thing my mother taught me was to always place plenty of emphasis on your spiritual soul, then that which is embedded in the mind will show in the spirit in a cool manner, with a high in emotional reactions. People like this are not afraid to speak of religion, and they are very friendly. One thing I try to remember is that there are some things and people you cannot change, but you can change your personality.

You have to live somewhere, some place in the world. No matter what race you are, you have to have shelter and a home. We are Americans who live a good, lavish life with our big cars, big houses, a lot of land, and plenty of trees. From the time you graduate from college, you start prospecting your dream; after graduating you learn the dream may cost you too much. So, you redesign your dream. When I lived in the country with the blue jays and red birds, I could not help but want to be around the fruit trees, with space and a lot of quietness, where people are more friendly, more giving, and will volunteer. They are much hap-pier. Is it more oxygen in the air, more trees? It was truly my domain. Living in the country, you enjoy every aspect of country living: the snakes you get use to, nights with the lightening bugs, the beetles, love bugs, and beautiful butterflies. I, myself, could not adjust to the fast life, the tall buildings, cars, bumper to bumper traffic, and sidewalks of people. I think everyone should fulfill his or her dream, but do not set the expectations too high and go where you are not wanted.

Your dreams may not come true, but what is wrong with dreaming? This is what motivates you each day. There are places in your society that may throw negative forces toward you to prevent your dream from coming true; but when this happens, do not stop dead in your tracks. All you have to do is reset your goal and continue to pursue your dream. Most of the time you will find that a negative person only sees pessimism, because this person has no goals and never set any goals, so there are no dreams for them.

When I was eighteen, I would drive around in subdivisions to get ideas for my dream home. At the time it was a good idea, you can accumulate ideas and develop your dream home. There were places that I would have loved to live, but because of my color, we were not invited to live in these neighborhoods because whites lived there. In the south, in the country, blacks living next to whites is common, but this will not happen in the city. There is a border line. So, I reset my goals.

I can make my castle wherever I go. Even living in a slum area, you can make your home wherever you are.

Sometimes it can be very difficult to live in an environment where bullets are flying around you. You make adjustments where you have to. There are some incidents that one cannot make adjustments for, so you have to develop other strategies.

What is wrong with America's tax system? It was designed by the upper class, and it doesn't affect them because they are on another tax level. America is only concerned about money. People's feelings mean nothing to America. Laws are designed to affect, not protect, the people.

This is not right; this is why we have problems in America. Everybody does not want to be on food stamps. Everybody does not want to be on Medicare. The old should be tax free. They will pay taxes until they die, and if they owe the government will take their house because of our outrageous tax laws. Before it is all over, we brainwash our citizens about unity and democracy. We are a devastating country. We are going the other way, then we wonder why we have militia groups. It is because we do not resolve our major issues.

Americans are putting fear into their citizens with their tax laws. Actually, I wonder if Red Foxx's death would have happened if his taxes would have been handled differently? The way they handle people may cause sickness; the Internal Revenue Service operates like communism. America in a non-biased fashion, not camouflaged by empowerment, or satanic or racial bigotry, atheism, and homosexuality. This is what a citizen is facing in our society.

What happened in Ruby Ridge, Waco, and Oklahoma City should not have happened; we have a tendency to push things aside for so long, hoping they will work themselves out. But, if we do not diffuse the bomb, sooner or later it is going to explode; when it does, the innocent will be ones to suffer.

Sometimes we have to contain our feelings to keep from releasing our prejudice. I realize that everybody on earth has some type of prejudice, but we must contain it.

Sometimes when things happen in a family, they cause many hardships for the mother, father, and the children-especially when kids see that there is an honest family. Notice, no wrongdoing from father and mother! It makes them grow-up with a negative attitude toward the government.

When our kids didn't have things like school tuition and clothes for school, they noticed everything that was happening to my wife, which was caused by the I.R.S. Personally, I feel that the people who work in the Internal Revenue Office enjoy their work. I do not set the blame on some of them, but our government allows them to do this. They make the rules that apply to our citizens. The employees just follow through on their orders. The I.R.S. needs to set up an office to investigate all internal revenue audits, especially those that are critical, to see what is happening to American families. They need to see what it is doing to families. I know, when they audited my family, how it changed my family's financial structure. We neglected many bills, and it made it difficult for to attend to the kids' health. When something needed fixing on the car, I could not fix it; I drove the car that way.

I recall when I drove my car without safety inspections for more than a year. It was difficult because when I pulled up to a light, I would not pull on the side of a police car, because he would see it was past due for inspection. I would always make it a point to never pull up beside a car at a light, because the driver might see something. I recall driving my car with the brake light on for weeks. I could not afford to buy brake fluid, so I would drive slowly and as I got to a stop sign or a red light, I would pump up the brakes until the light went off. This would let me know that the pressure was up. I know that I was jeopardizing other people's lives, but I needed my job so I could pay the taxes and feed my family.

At the same time, my daughter was in college; she was in nursing, and she had to work at the hospital. The car had bad tires, so after a couple of blow outs, we had to park the car until we could get the money to buy some used tires. My daughter borrowed her grandmother's car. It had a bad gas leak, so I had to improvise because I did not have any money. I got some number-eight tread and stopped the gas leak. When times are rough, you learn how to survive, even though you are endangering your family and other citizens. I recall riding on balloon tires for over a year. What I would do was let the air out of the tire, and this would cause the tire to level out enough to where I would get a smooth ride. I recall once when I had a bad alternator, and my battery would go low. I would park the old Chevy on a hill at the house and let it roll down to start. When I went to pay a bill, I would leave the car motor running. I could not, as you can see, live the American dream. I was punished because at the time of my business, during inflation, I borrowed money from my thrift to keep the business going. However, I paid the penalty interest anyway. There were many times when I bought used tires to keep me with transportation. If I would not have known how to do certain mechanical repairs, I would have never survived. Extra bills would cause something else not to be paid. Sometimes I wonder, if I were a foreigner in this country, would I get all these bad breaks?

I remember that a foreigner once told me, "I get better breaks than you do, and you have been in this country all your life. I just got here, and I am treated better. You have to pay taxes, work hard, and fight for this country, and you cannot live where you want to. I was tough, and I am conditioned for all types of torture. I remember what the Indians went through; the Jews made me much tougher, and I know what it will take for me and my family to survive in this country. The reason why less blacks commit suicide is because of what black families have already gone through. From childhood, they are taught by their parents to deal with difficult situations. When there were difficulties, even in slavery, blacks found ways to cope by singing hymns. I remember many nights when my family was hungry. There were times when I would miss a meal so the family could eat the remainder of the food left in the pot.

There were many other chores that I had to do because we did not have money. One was installing the clutch on the car. All mechanical work had to be performed by me, because we could not afford it. Not having enough money to function causes one to live on the edge. For three years I knew that my furnace was leaking monoxide; I knew the central unit needed to be replaced. At the time I was hoping the money to fix it would come, but it did not. Since I was not sure, I got a friend to look at it and inspect the unit. He found that the burners were all plugged up. Rust and corrosion inside the units were causing the burners to be plugged. This caused some of the burners to burn, and the others were smothered and caused monoxide to form. I took a chance; there were many times when we would not use the heater, because sometimes gas would build up and cause a small explosion before the heater would come on.

Situations such as these are just what can happen when a family is put into conditions that they cannot afford. You pay your back taxes; that is forced upon you, creating a bad financial dilemma. I had to learn to put up with an empty refrigerator. When I got hungry, all I had to do was eat a slice of bread, drink water, and go to bed. Now when I have a little change, I go to the store, get three packs of thirty-five cent corn bread mix, and fix myself some cush, cush-milk, and cornbread. This is the poor man's rib-eye. When you live in poverty for so long, a Coke is a bottle of champagne.

When money is not available, you learn how to buy your bread at thrift stores and get your fruit and eggs from fruit stands. If I went by my mother's house, she fed me a full meal. She would do this because she noticed I was losing a lot of weight. When my mother fed me, I would not worry about eating another meal, because I can survive on one meal a day.

When I would go to church on Sunday, I always made it a point to sit where there were not too many people around so I would not feel embarrassed because I did not have money to put into the collection. Sometimes I would fold a dollar to make it appear I was putting a lot into the collection.

My buddy wanted to know who cut my hair. I told him a barber shop; but really, I could not afford a barber shop. I just did not have the money. There were many times I scared myself, because when I shaved with a mirror looking backwards, I thought I had cut a mole behind my neck. That really scared me.

Sometimes when things happen to you, you learn how to improvise. Our chairs and recliners were gone; so I went to the fabric shop and bought myself some leather material for it and began to rip off the old material. I got a staple gun and put the recliner together. Then my neighbors across the street put a recliner in the garbage; we got it, stripped it down, and cleaned it up. I fixed it with a few screws, and we had a new chair in our living room.

The only thing I could not fix in the house was the refrigerator. It would freeze up sometimes. At other times it would not freeze at all. After having it for so many years, the plastic had cracked and allowed hot air to get inside, causing the box to freeze up. There are many things we did to survive, like taking a light bulb out one room to use in another.

My daughter felt sorry for me and bought me a lawn mower, because she was afraid the motor was going to come off in the old mower. The mower base that held the motor corroded, causing the blade to be exposed, slinging out the rocks, and sometimes the motor would tremble, creating vibrations which would cause the motor to come off.

I have always felt like I did not belong in this United States because of the way I have been treated. After living like this, we usually contribute to organizations such as the fire fighters, United Givers, and police organizations. The phone would ring all of the time; but I explained to them what was happening to my family that caused us to be living on the edge. We would be better off robbing a bank; then my family would no longer have to suffer.

I suddenly realized that once someone starts working with the mind, this will control the person the continuous sending of letters with information on how the interest continuously adds up, and the next thing is to put a lien against your property. This is a scare tactic that can force a person to do whatever it takes for the person's family to survive. This can mess with your health. It can cause certain chemicals to secrete, causing a person to develop an ulcer. It has caused people to have nerve problems, which could develop into something that could cause headaches-migraine headaches. This was happening to me because of the worry about what tomorrow would bring and what was going to happen next.

These tactics are a continuous thing that has been happening to me over the past eight to ten years. This is why worry can kill you. It can cause swelling in blood vessels, an aneurysm, a stroke, and also a heart attack. So, I guess it is all right for the government to play Russian Roulette with our lives; the only thing that is important to this country is money. After all of this, we see hospitals trying to rehabilitate the person to try to get their health back, so they can go back and pay some more taxes. After retirement, when the end is near, we need to figure out how we can get our retirement money. The things that happen in life are not caused by the government. Sometimes it is forced upon you by others. Some people have feelings, and some people are never bothered. It reminds me of a criminal that commits a crime, and it never bothers him. Sometimes, auditors never realize what powers they have and how abusive it could be on other families. If they could read my wife's health report, then they could see what sadness and pain they inflict upon others.

The feeling of sadness, the fear of life and death, the unknown, the uncertainty: regardless of my near-death experience, the fear is still there. The feeling of your loved ones going through so much pain and suffering you always say, why? But who really knows? When sickness occurs, the loved ones suffer as much as the individual who is sick. When I go to mass, I sit in the pews that were once for blacks who were segregated from the rest of the church. The reason I sit there is because no one wants to sit there because of what it used to be like. I sit there because I do not want anyone to see me crying. I have been going into those moods that put me into a sad state. I think about my being honest all my life and what the result of my life is now. Was it worth it? I think about how I sacrificed my virginity all those years, because I wanted to be true to my wife, because of what my father had done to his family. The next thing, the priest always says something that refers directly to what is happening or has happened to me. Your mind plays tricks with you. You think of a friend who grew up with you and how his or her life was totally different. And how he or she had nothing happen like what had happen to you. Then you want to know, why?

I remember on Father's Day, I wanted to cry because I had no father. A friend of my family, who had the ideal family, would gather up everything on the weekend and go picnicking and fishing with his father and mother, and I could not. It hit a low blow on me. I would go home, climb into the bed in my room, play music, and try to get rid of the thought; but it continued to come back-that lonesome part of my life that was missing.

I continue to believe in God and have faith, because man has to make adjustments in life where he has to. Sometimes in life things will happen, and no one will ever understand why. All we can do is pray for things to get better. I did, but each time things got worse. My father left my mother when I was three weeks old. I wondered whether it was because of me. Why did this happen to my family? A child with-out a father misses so much as to folkways. The next thing was finding out what my father did to me that almost caused my death. Was it infatuation, or was it the animal that is in men-the desire to have someone or just lust? The next thing was when I finally got a stepfather, God had something else planned for him. I tried to be a man at twelve years old. I tried to become a part of the peer group in school; I was rejected there. One boy in the group rejected me. He just burst me in the mouth for no reason whatsoever. Right after my stepfather died, I really could not accept anyone as a friend. Then I realized that my own race did not want to have anything to do with me, so I would always go off by myself and try to find peace, even though I had brothers who were much older than I. I still experienced rejection; I became a loner and found other ways to occupy myself. The feeling of sadness will continue to follow me. Do you still wonder why this life of Joseph Therance could not be any different? So I continue to cling closer to God. I never discussed this with my mother because she had enough problems.

When it came to sex and other things, it was hush, hush; you kept everything inward. When I entered into college, I thought it would be different, because on the collegiate level we had a different class of people. Their level of understanding was supposed to be higher, but I still experienced some rejection by instructors who probably had a reason for their rejection; they experienced the same from families who were also white. There were black families that had a Spanish-white look, who would not marry or allow dark-skinned people into their families. They had a reason when they saw me with a light-skinned person to conceive the wrong thing. It got so bad that I decided to stop school, and I did. I got drafted into the army and still experienced the same from the blacks from Philadelphia, Chicago, California, and all over the United States. I still experienced the same rejection by both races. At first, it continued with my own race, but I got to the point where I had to get rid of this fear; I decided I was going to break the barrier. When I would run into a group of black guys, I would ignore prejudice. Now I know the fear will continue, because as long as man exists there will be fears. The next fear I thought would never happen to me. It was what happened to me in the Internal Revenue Office. When one lives with prejudice for so long, you get to the point you can feel it when you enter a room. The negative forces hit you, and you say to yourself, "This is not happening! This is not true!" You trust the person and go ahead with what you expect the person to do. But later, you realize your instinct was right all the time.

Because of your faith in God and mankind, you still wake up each day and anticipate a change to come. That one morning, you think that God must have touched each person, that the earth has a touch of heaven; but his moment of peace was only for four brief seconds. Then the fear approaches you from another angle, like a snake hiding in the bush-es. But this time, the Therances's were going to experience another type of fear, and that was a materialistic fear. One can ask, "How much can one bear?" This time my family was going to feel it-my children, after losing my store; then my brother, dying I was already filled all the way up to my nose. A little more fear would drown my faith. Then I would go to church and try to participate in the mass. Once again the feeling, choking, and the sadness reappeared.

You wonder, "Why me, God?" But God had nothing to do with this. I know this was the work of the devil. Once again, I would sit in mass and wonder why. Then I would think this to be just life, and I had to believe that everybody in life was going through the same phenomena. But deep down inside of me, I knew it was not so. I would take a deep breath, sit out by the City Park Lake, or pray while driving my car to change my expression. When I approached my mother, she could see what was happening to me inside. As you know, one cannot fool his or her mother. They can see through expressions, because a smile is a facade over one's faith. The eyes can reveal the inner feeling of an individual that is really hurting inside. So mother would ask what was wrong, and then I would finally break down and tell the truth about what was happening in my life and how I was losing each day. She would try to always bring God into the picture and ask me to read Psalms, and once I talked to her, I would feel a lot better. But I had to stop telling Mother, because it was having an affect on her health. This is why sometimes we have to bite our lip before saying something to avoid infringing on the rights of others.

This time I thought that luck was finally coming my way. We had lost the store, property, apartment, and our home. The worst thing that can ever happen to a person is to lose his health. I heard someone say that when a person loses his property, the next thing for him is his health, and this happened to my wife. When I retired because of my wife's bad health, after her health began deteriorating so quickly, I thought it was all over for her; but she came back. I got happy a little too soon. She went back to work and was doing really well. Then she became worse than the first time. She had three seizures. This caused me to go back into my house of fears. This time I was more scared than before. I had to have a long talk with God. I realized that my wife was holding on to this earth with the tip of her fingers, and the gravity from heavens was pulling her away from this earth. I knew that it was time for me to get closer to God; then other things happened, just at the time we thought she would be going back to work. She found out that her best friend had given her job to someone else, and she was sitting home with a face full of tears and a heart full of fire. She put the blame on her health. She had prayed to God that she would not lose her job; then it did happen. When the word got out that she had a stroke on her spine, she knew her best friend would be calling her; but she never got a call, not even a card. I told her that people change when dealing with money-friendship is one thing, and money is another. Some people worship money like a god. So, the fears have never escaped me. After seeing my wife's body being punctured so many times with needles and so much blood being drawn, you would think she did not have any left; but her faith was full of positive attitudes with Jesus and all the angels at her side. I have to quit looking over my shoulder and look for the Blood of Jesus. Instead, I should look for the Roses and the sweet smell of sweetness.

From the time of childbirth, from changing diapers, feeding, cleaning me, and working outside, she never stopped taking care of me. Mother had two roles after my real father left me when I was three weeks old. She maintained the family herself.

When I was a child, she would take my father's old suits, rip them apart, re-cut the material, and make me a suit. All we needed to buy were shoes. In all the turmoil that she went through, she stuck by her kids. When we moved to Baton Rouge, she knew how to save. Things others would throw away, like water melon rinds, she would save and preserve in jars. She would do the same with figs. We always had enough food because we would grow vegetables from the garden. Mother would preserve vegetables and tomatoes. We always had enough food.

Nineteen forty was a year of peace and harmony around our home, but the country was in war at that time. I was too young to know what was happening. Mother was a person who would hustle. She would make flowers using pet milk cans, and I would sell them. She would make roses out of crepe paper, and she would buy wax from the hardware store, melt the wax on the gas stove, and dip the flowers so they would be preserved. We would make chrysanthemums, gladiolas, and carnations when special holidays approached, such as Mother's Day. This was a special occasion. You would see everybody wearing their red corsages on their lapels, white ones if their parents were dead. People today do not do this like they did during the old days. Twice we faced conditions that were fatherless, but mother maintained her sanity and continued her loyal support, playing both roles, as mother and father. Both brothers had left home when my stepfather died, so it created a situation where I had to grow up fast.

Mothers always fulfill the obligation of providing all the conveniences. They wipe your tears from your eyes, comfort you when you cry, keep you warm in the winter, keep you clean all the time, provide you with shelter, and keep your bed clean. The same occurs for me now in all that I have gone through. My mother gives me hope, faith, and love. If Mother had not been there, I probably would have committed suicide, because at times I could not see the purpose of life. When one has lost everything, the next thing to go is one's health. My mother showed me that, even though you have lost everything, you still have something for which to live. You have your family, and this is what mother explained to me the true purpose of life, and how the things that government may do defy the laws of nature and survival.

Mothers never stop comforting their children. I watched my moth-er when my brother was sick. She comforted my brother when he was in his sixties and never stopped trying to nurse him back to health. When my brother died, I watched my mother mourning and trying to shake life back into him; my mother took it hard. There were a few mornings when I would go to see her, and she would have been crying. She had a hard time adjusting to the death of her child. One time I watched a tiger mourn the death of her little one. She would howl, mourning the death, and would drag the cub and bury the newborn. Even animals mourn the death of a loved one.

My mother is eighty-five years old, with all of her faculties, and still fulfilling her role as mother. In the final phase of my life, when I was about to leave this earth, she gave me the special treatment. She supplied me with comfort and gave me a new insight on life. Sometimes people are victims of circumstances that are beyond their control. Those people empowered themselves to play God, ruined my life, and caused my family suffering, pain, and sickness that almost led to the death of my wife. At the time when all this happened, my mother would pray for me, pro-vide me emotional and financial support, and offer me with good meals. What more can a mother do for her child? She puts him into the world, nourishes him, feeds him, and watches him go into the ground.

After I lost my home Mother got angry, because I did not try to tell her I needed money to keep from losing my home; but I did not want burden her with my problem. As you know, when a family goes through what happened to me, you do not want your family to suffer. I kept everything to myself.

I have always believed that any time a situation creates a bad dilemma for an American family, then something is wrong with the system: taking a home from an American family because they got behind on their taxes and giving this home to foreigners, closing their business down because they got behind on their taxes and helping to put foreigners into the same business, allowing them so many years without paying taxes. My mother could not understand how this government could take the food out of the mouth of the person who had fought for and helped to build this country, then when they get old the government denies them certain benefits. Like one fight promoter said, "Only in America."

Born of the blood of the United States of America-this means that you are an American. I never could understand how people in Mexico are considered Mexicans. Why is it when blacks are born in America, they have to be characterized according to their color, while a white American, who may be a descendent of another country, is still recognized as part of this country? They are characterized as white Americans no matter how much Italian, Jewish, Polish, or any other nation's blood in them, except black. They are characterized as Afro-Americans, because they do not belong in this country. If they did belong, they would be called Americans like the white man, not Afro. No part of this country is a part of Africa. Other nationalities are characterized as white on birth certificates. We have to change the image and the laws of this country that put its own citizens in denial. When the constitution was written, the blacks of this country were in slavery. Was the constitution written for slaves? I do not think so; the laws were only written for the white citizens. It discriminated against women and blacks. I cannot believe in a country that is in modern times, approaching the new era, that we are still living in an old era; then we wonder why we are having so much trouble in this country.

It is because of the way the laws are written. They discriminate, not only against the old citizens, but against those who still are the forefathers of this country.

When that flag flies with the red, white, and blue, it represents a small amount of Americans. For a very long time, there was a demand for a change in the country. Eyes were closed upon the main issues of this country because the old diehards would not let it happen. This is what is preventing this country from progressing. We thought we did so much by going to the moon, but we have not been able to conquer this earth where we are living today.

We have closed our eyes on so many issues that we have denied certain citizens to be recognized as a full-fledged citizens. How long is it going to take? Will it take another hundred years for common sense to prevail? When you watch a fruit tree grow, you cut the dead limbs; you keep the weeds from growing around it. And then when it needs water, you provide it. When it does not grow, you provide it with fertilizer. Then it grows with dark green leaves and bares a tremendous fruit, and you suddenly realize that to have this form of unity, you have to provide all aspects that are required to make good fruit. A government operates on the same principle, and this is not done in a gradual process. You have to move rapidly, because time goes on and no progress is made, and that is what is happening in America today. We are evading the main issues.

You cannot expect this nation to progress by living in the same one hundred years of law. We have to recognize that our constitution is dis-criminating against its citizens, so it needs some revisions. We are living in modern times with all the old laws. What should happen if the United States throws away color and recognizes all its people as one. What would happen if this government changed it's tax laws and made it equal for everyone? Our laws are for the will of the majority. What would happen is this country would treat their citizens the same as they treat foreigners in this country?

As our laws are revised, we will begin to see progress. When our politicians to speak out with discrimination against another race, these politicians should be banned from public office. This is a betrayal of trust. If we do not change our laws, we will be beyond the year 2000 and yet still behind one hundred years. Why can't we deal directly with the issues? It is because we have for so long closed our eyes and been hush-hush about everything.

The main problem with America is that we need to deal directly with the issue, like a virus invading the country. Money is the problem of this country. It is more important than the truth. Making enough money-that is the important thing in this country. How can we take the home of someone who is troubled and whose family is distressed and expect this country to run smoothly? How can we take food from a troubled family in return for money? This causes sickness in a family. Now I know what "United we stand, divided we fall means, because my family has been tortured and drained of blood. The only thing we have left is a withered bone structure that is still trying to survive in all the confusion. We are not born mathematicians to understand the tax laws; yet when we go to the tax office, they do not have the time to explain it to us. They do not understand it themselves.

How long is it going to take for the government to know that we need changes quickly? Time is passing. We cannot clean up our own environment; we cannot help the homeless. Yet we can provide assistance for foreigners coming into this country. There is an epidemic hanging over this country; we are again closing our eyes to drugs. At the rate drugs have entered into this country, we could do something about it, but because of money no one knows anything about it. I know what is going on. We know that it is the little people on the street who are being arrested, but they are not the ones who should be arrested.

The ones who have the money to buy drugs are not my next-door neighbors; they are members of large organizations. They are the people who are top members of a church. They are the ones shown in your Sunday paper in the aristocratic society, members of the country club, presidents of large corporations, and members of political parties. There are people who are serving the public, keeping everything hush-hush from the public for a very long time. We have been watergating in this country for a very long time; we see so much in this country that the younger generation will not know who to trust. How long is it going to take for this country to wake up to the facts and clean up the part of our society that really stinks? The country needs a lot of cleaning up. I won- der, what would happen if the drugs and crime were stopped? What would happen if we got the homeless off the street? What would happen if we stopped the drugs from coming into this country? Would our schools get better? Would we produce more scientists, engineers, doctors, lawyers, and teachers? After the year 2000, will our country have made more progress toward science or maybe even a cure for cancer or AIDS? So you see, what we do every day is a part of our destiny if we continue in this direction. The way we are going now, we will destroy mankind.

Are things happening which you are not aware of because of your environment? So many things happen to which you are not paying attention. Or is it just a coincidence? Are you just a victim of circumstances? When we have bad luck, do we look for the next thing to happen? Many things happen in your environment that cannot be explained; but then no matter how much you know or how well educated you are, man is there. There are spooky things that happen at my home, or in the area of my home. This was a home that was built from the ground up. We know that there were too many things that happened in the area where we lived. Was it a coincidence, or were there some forces of life that we could not ever understand?

When a toilet flushes more than one time, the logical explanation would be that the rubber flap dry rotted, causing the water to leak through the float, come down, and flush the toilet automatically. That is the logical explanation; but what I did let me know that there was some- thing else going on in the area. I went to the hardware store and bought all new equipment to repair the toilet. We replaced the flap with a new one and checked the float to see if it had a pin hole in it. It had no water in it, and it was in good shape. I got my tools out, cleaned all trash inside the toilet, washed inside the toilet, and proceeded to replace the flap. I put the water on, let the tank fill up, and flushed the toilet to see if the water was leaking, and causing the toilet to flush. We tried it over and over again. The toilet never malfunctioned; we knew the toilet was working properly. That night I knew I would get some sleep. Early in the morning, the toilet flushed, and as the tank was filling up with water, it again flushed. It would not flush anymore that night; so was this normal? You be the judge.

The next incident I never told my wife or kids about, because I did not want to scare them. At first, I thought it was a nightmare, but then I realized my eyes were open. It felt like someone was on top of me with a heavy weight, and I could not move it. It was like when I was a child and my brother was playing with me, holding my hands and arms down and sitting on top of me. I could not move at all, rolling from side to side.

I could not remove the weight from my body, and I just fell asleep. When I woke up again, it was gone away. The incident happened again; this time I felt like hands were around my throat and fingers around my neck. It was choking me, and I could not breathe. I woke up gasping for air like I was totally out of breath.

We hear things happening, and there is always someone to question what happens. When my wife called me at the store and told me that some human-like figure walked through the house, she claimed it was a tall man in a black outfit walking through the house. My daughter came in and asked her mother if she had seen the man who walked through the house. That was the first time this happened. My wife never told me about that, until one day she was talking to someone and told them what had happened and told them that we had a rest from the strange phenomena.

The other neighbors were not having the same problems that we were having. It always centered around us. Was this some form of magnetic field, or was it something for which man does not have an explanation?

We had a storage shed that was lifted up and put next to the bedroom window. Limbs from trees, from high winds which usually just blow leaves from the trees, would be all over the ground. The pine needles were not on the ground after high winds, and no objects from the fence were removed. This was a redwood fence. No shingles were removed from the roof. The weather was clear with no bad weather expected. It was a sudden noise, and it was not wind that removed that storage shed. I believe it was something strange that happened that man cannot explain. We rolled the shed back into place. Another year the same thing happened with the same phenomena.

This time whatever it was did the same thing and disintegrated the storage shed. I knew then that something was wrong. This was something beyond the ordinary; who says that electricity does not strike the same place twice. Well, I know that where we lived the trees were chopped off at the top, and the trees did not die. The next time my wife called me at the store and told me the electricity was traveling across the yard, I denied what she told me and ignored her. I knew this did not happen to anyone else in the neighborhood. But the electricity did what she said it was doing, traveling back and forth; it was marked on four trees. It took all the bark off the trees and split portions of them, and some sap came out the trees. If I would take someone there, the mark of what happened is still there. A school teacher told me about a little girl who lived in the house who had a sudden change in personality. She agreed with me because of the instant change in the little girl's personality. There is something going on that is beyond the ordinary.

Everybody born on this earth has a purpose. It is given to them as soon as they are born. God has given them life on earth with a purpose and an obligation. Everything on earth should be done religiously. When I was born on this earth, I was awakened one morning with images of things that I had never before seen. It was the earth. As years went by, I found out that everything was not done religiously, that there were a lot of evil forces on this earth. Being raised in a family that was highly religious gave me the proper roots for religious rearing. When I was six years old, I would read the Bible and act as though I was a preacher, because I really wanted to be a preacher. For some reason as I got older, I got sidetracked with peers and being with a group of boys, doing boyish things. But as I became a teenager thing changed, causing me to get sidetracked again. With my sickness, I realized what I had and the dan-ger involved, and this caused me to get closer to God once again. I prayed really hard late at night while in the hospital. I asked God to spare my life because I was too young. Looking out of the window at the hospital, seeing people going to work, I asked God to let me just be like one of them-healthy-and to allow me to live a long life and let me walk out of that hospital healthy once again. God answered my prayer. Just ask and you shall be given, and it was given.

When I was a teenager, I weighed about fifty pounds soaking wet. I did not have many friends, and I did not have a girlfriend. They cared only for the guys who played football. I did not have a chance because I did not possess the qualities that the muscle men possessed. After my near-death experience, God answered my prayer once again. It was a miracle that happened for me. I was allowed to walk out of the hospital, and God allowed me to be one of those people who were going to work in the morning, those I watched from the window of my hospital room. I know that for a man to get his prayers answered, he must be a believer in God and must follow God's rules. You must humble yourself to him, because he is your only Father. You have to show respect to Him. Remember, you cannot hide from God. God is one friend who will never leave you alone.

When my stepfather died, I saw my family was splitting up, and my mother was falling apart. I prayed to God to please help me and my moth-er to survive. I asked him to help me to be a man at eleven and to stick hy my mother. When she was crying one day in the kitchen, God put words into my mind that told me what to say to my mother to spring her back into the world. God gave me the magic words that I said: "God loaned everybody upon this earth." What God did turned a cry into a smile, and from that day until now my mother is still smiling. She is now eighty-four. Everything that it was done by God. I truly understand how God operates, and we do not realize that we are sometimes messengers of God. He comes to us during the day, and sometimes he comes in a dream.

I remember one time when I was very young, I had a friend who died. It scared me because I was so young. This was something that did not happen to young people. Young people do not die, only old people. There were many lonesome nights when I would walk the streets, because I was afraid that I was going to die. I really had a strong fear of death. There were times when I would take my mind so far that a blank spot would appear. I would see nothing. It seemed like life, for me, had made a sudden stop. And I would holler, "O God, help me!" I would get up, take a walk, and try to get death off my mind. I heard that when one is lonesome, the mind begins to play tricks and can in turn cause suicide. Sometimes people are just too anxious to see what is on the other side.

I did not know what had happened to me after praying to God to remove the fear of death from me so I could live a normal, happy life without the fear of the unknown. Then one day after this prayer to God, there was a show on near-death experiences; then it hit me. All this time, the fear I felt was the fear of death. I did not know, because I thought it was something else. But in later years, I finally knew that it did happen; suddenly I realized that God did spare me. It really made me take a different outlook on life.

Some people have a very small encounter with God because of the materialistic world in which they live. Society advertises only for commercializing for money. In college they build you up with such a high esteem with fraternities and sororities; after graduating we find out that it is different once we get out in the real world. They blow things totally out of proportion; they leave out the most essential part of life, and that is God.

The universities need a course in religion. This can put man in a true relation with God. Man has a tendency to live in values with no relationship to God. Sometimes man gets too educated; then he thinks he is smarter than God. He professes there is no God. He wants to emphasize that science is what makes man. He really does not believe in God. But if that man had been where I have been, then he would become a true believer.

The things that happened to me make me know that there is some supreme being that is truly in charge of what is and what is to be. For me to wake up one morning in the world with a life, mind, body, and spirit, there are some forces out there that are much stronger than any machine, computer, or any other type of sophisticated operation. What God gives man-and he uses a little of-is common sense.

The University does not teach common sense. It just gives you a general education. I, myself, have always put God first in my life. Man cannot leave God out of his life. What happened in my early childhood led me to become an early believer in God-from a near-death experience to the death of my grandmother, father, and brother. My wife's health is very bad; instead of praying for her health, she told me she prayed that God would remove the Internal Revenue Service from the burden of our family. Then she also prayed that we could once again be a family. She prayed for a house that has two stories, but God did not answer that prayer for a reason. God knew then that she would never walk again, so living upstairs would make it difficult to transport her up and down the stairs. God had something else planned for her. The thing God was going to do; He would do it all together.

When I pray to God, I always ask him to show me a sign to know that he is answering my prayer. That sign only God and I would under-stand; however, He gave me everything all together at once. The house we wanted was really well organized and small-ideal for what we need-ed. My wife, being paralyzed and using a wheelchair, had a patio in the rear, with plenty of space for her to be able to maneuver her wheelchair.

This house was to be bought by her first cousin. They were to meet at the lawyer's office to sign the papers and finalize the sale of the property. A young man driving a stolen truck ran into the house, causing fifteen thousand dollars' worth of damage. Well, she changed her mind about the house. Then my mother-in-law called and talked to the owner of the house. God touched this gentleman. He told her for me to call him, and he would give me an offer that I could not refuse. It did hap-pen. I got tears in my eyes; this was the beginning of how God operates. After the offer of a home for my wife, that same day I got a call from someone else who God touched. They gave me the money for the house. I went to the hospital to tell my wife what had happened. It was like waking up to a new Christmas with lots of goodies. When I told my wife the news, she smiled and cried at the same time. For the first time in about eight to ten years, we felt like citizens with those certain rights that we should have been getting all the time. While my wife was smiling and crying at the same time, the phone rang. There was another member of my family offering assistance to help a family that had been tortured for so long. We then got another phone call from a finance company, a lady who God told to call me. I explained that we had only a Small retirement checks are coming, and we were barely surviving. This lady told me she understood what my family's circumstances were like. Since my wife was disabled, this case was under hardship.

The next day I went to see my lawyer to discuss what we needed for handling the closing costs. God touched my lawyer; he refused to accept any money. He did this out of the goodness of his heart, with the touch of God. I wondered if something bad was going to happen, because this was something I wasn't used to, but the surprise was a call from the owner of a community home health organization. She claimed she had some insurance papers that I needed for a disability claim from the finance company. While driving along the highway, there was a manila folder on the seat. I decided to open it; there was a check in there for eight thousand dollars for my wife. We had just moved out of the apartment, not knowing where the funds would come from to pay the utility bill, telephone bill, truck rental for moving, plus the cost of the washing machine and refrigerator. Things never stopped happening. Like I said before, I asked God to show me a sign when He answered my prayer. If He does something, He will do a large amount of things for me all together; that is the sign. He put me in a position where I could recognize how quickly He answers or creates a situation where those who come in my path would have experienced the same phenomena. They would talk about the situation, and that would ease my mind.

When my wife was in the hospital, I met a family who had a similar sickness as my wife. The man told me what to expect and how to cope. The other instance was the lady at the finance company who told me of a similar situation that happened to someone who was close to her. Once again, she advised me to get home health services, what to do to get help, and how to read about Christ in difficult times.

Prayer is the answer! For a long time when I was small, I would hear old people talk about prayers being the answer. Being young, I did not understand because I was of the next generation. I did not listen because they were old fashioned. But now that I am older, I understand more about prayers being the answer to all situations in life.

The purpose of churches, priests, ministers, and the Bible is similar to the Bill of Rights- they set the rules for life. The church keeps man together, as well as his family. The priests and ministers are the leaders of the earth. They are the doctors of Christianity.

I think when one person prays, it helps a person with problems. When my wife was ill, we had prayers coming from a large amount of people. It is a known fact that healing takes place when a large number of a congregation or family get together and pray. Then healing takes place. The person who is ill, however, must want to be healed. They have to straighten their soul out to totally commit to God. One has to remember, always, to put God first in everything he or she does.

When my wife was in the hospital, the doctors claimed they had never seen any patient with such a positive attitude as my wife. She told the doctor that she would walk again. She would pray all during the night and ask relatives to pray for her. I, myself, could not pray because of my mixed emotions. In my mind, I knew that Lupus was deadly.

My wife complained about not having any feeling in the lower part of her body and around her breast. You could not touch her because of the pain she was having. While in the hospital, one of the aids came in to give her a bath. She had brought in a pitcher of water. She removed the sheets and touched her left foot, and my wife jumped and told her that her hands were cold. The aid was fascinated and said that this could be a good sign. Maybe her feet were coming back! But I did not expect anything to happen. My wife continued to take therapy, and she was finally discharged. They told her what the chances were of her walking again. She answered them, saying that could be taken two ways-yes and no. With God, I have always believed anything can happen.

There was another doctor I talked with who was a psychologist. We had a long talk, and he believed the same thing I believed. We talked for about an hour, and he told me when I got my wife home, to get her to close her eyes and imagine that she was healed. Then he said to try feeling her foot and sending messages to different parts of her body, starting with the lower part. That night, I asked her to send messages, like telling her foot and toes to move. We did this for a long time, but nothing ever happened; this disappointed her. On another visit to the doctor, the neurologist took a pin, stuck her toes, and asked her if she felt it. There was no sensation, but my wife kept a positive attitude.

There were good and bad mornings. I would sometimes feel so badly for her; my emotions would get the best of me. I did not want to let her see me breaking down; so I would go out on the patio, hide behind the curtain, and cry my heart out. I tried to pull myself back together before I faced her again. I did not want her to see me sad, because this would not help her healing. For healing to take place, the environment must be joyful; we had to talk about positive things, and it had to smell as sweet as a rose. There were times that I bit my lip when she would be grouchy, but I always thought about what it would be like if I was in her place. I would probably act the same. I continued talking to her, telling her to exercise by getting up each morning, to get out of bed and into the wheelchair. This required physical activity that would prevent her from getting stiff. The doctors kept a continuous watch on the steroids, because steroids can activate other illnesses that could have a bearing on the healing process.

My wife continued on the steroids and chemotherapy; during this time, she developed bladder infections. Sometimes, she would break down and cry, and healing cannot take place if you do not control your emotions; so, I would work on her emotions once again. Everybody in the family would give her so much support that she would come out of the negative mode and get back on track once again. During the day we would give her exercise by moving her legs, and this persisted for a given period of time. I could see an improvement in her personality, and during the night I would wake up and find her praying. Then one morning for breakfast, we talked about what we could do to alleviate certain problems she was having. She gave me a surprise. She told me that she was feeling sensations in her bladder. Sometimes she had feelings in her left leg, and sometimes the leg would have spasms. During the night I would find her leg hanging out of the side of the bed; the spasms would cause her left leg to move.

One morning my wife went to the clinic to see the doctor about taking chemotherapy, and God sent a little white lady who was also on chemotherapy. She had a friend along who drove her to the clinic. From the time she walked in, she never stopped talking. She kept observing my wife, because she noticed my wife was very worried. When she went for chemotherapy, she found out that her blood count was not right; she could not receive treatment. The lady came over, started talking to her, and explained that everything was going to be all right. She told her about how she thought she was going to die after having a stroke and seizure. One day she, too, decided she was again going to walk. She was sitting inside looking at her flower bed-how the grass was taking it over-and decided she was going outside to get some fresh air. She crawled to the front porch, lifted herself up, braced herself against the banister, raised herself up, and stood up. She said she felt like screaming; but being out-side was what motivated her to move forward. When her kids came home from school, they found her home laying in the flower bed getting dirty. She loved being outside. The dirt felt good to her. The wind blew through her hair; she smelled the freshness of the air and the warmth of the sun upon her skin. Once again, she felt like living.

When she got through talking, I saw a smile in my wife's eyes. I knew that God had given her the message that was needed to cheer her up. When we were leaving the clinic, she was coming out of the parking lot. The white angel lady got out of her van, came back to my wife, and gave her some more positive words. When we left the clinic, my wife was full of flame and fire. She was ready to get back on track and get back to solving her medical problems. When a person is having medical problems, he or she has to pay attention to many things, especially facial expressions and staring. You have to pay attention and react immediately. Sometimes a stare or an instant change in expression could be a sign that a seizure is developing. You have to talk to the per-son about pleasant things to change the mood of the individual. Since my wife had the stroke on her spine, we talked to several individuals who had experienced strokes. Some who had a positive attitude helped me because each day they looked forward to something positive happening to them. Each day I looked forward to something positive happening to her.

On October 28, 1997, I was getting ready to go into the kitchen to get some coffee when God told me to stop and try something. I went over to wife and asked her to close her eyes and to send messages for her toes to move. I noticed the toes moving slightly, but I was not sure. I told her that I thought her toes moved, and she thought her knees moved a little, not her toes. I asked her to try again. Her toes moved, and she said they had been moving all the time. I said, "No, they have not been moving all the time." She got excited and started crying and started to again move her toes. I started crying with joy. I asked her to move her right foot. Then she really got excited and started moving both feet. She never stopped crying. She must have cried for two hours. My daughters came in and wanted to know what the excitement was all about; my wife start-ed moving both of her feet. My daughters could not do anything but stare with joy on their faces. One of my daughters got on the phone and called my mother-in-law. She realized something good had happened.

It never dawned on us that something was happening that was impossible according to what the doctor had seen on the M.R.I. I thought about what the doctor had told me about why my wife was not having any feeling in the lower part of her body. The neurologist said the nerves had disconnected when the stroke occurred. My wife knew what happened. I never knew until after her movement occurred. She explained that she knew her prayers were answered. When she visited the neurologist, she asked the doctor if she had ever seen anyone that had a stroke heal like this, and she said, "No. You must have someone from above working for you." As a doctor for many years, she had never seen a person with a stroke heal after eight months. Usually, if the per-son has not shown any movement after two months, the patient is paralyzed for life. She admitted it had to be a miracle because the nerves never go back together. She said this was remarkable, the greatest thing she had ever seen. She was the first doctor to admit that God had to be the one; usually doctor's do not like to admit that God did the healing. They never talk about God around their patients. Only the person who has the experience can admit it had to be God.

After this the neurologist said she was going to put my wife in therapy. Things were arranged with our medical association, but it did not work the way we wanted. Once the neurologist made the call, weeks went by and then months, and nothing happened. I knew the devil was trying to stop progress. My wife called the nurse who worked for the doctor, and she would say everything had been taken care of, and then weeks went by again. My wife started giving up her faith and hope. My sister-in-law was talking with me about my wife entering into a state of depression. Then I went to the mailbox the next day, and there were letters from the Internal Revenue Service. I knew I needed to help her healing and not let things get her down. I took it upon myself to call Internal Revenue. I talked to the wrong person, a young black woman. She was not nice at all. She spoke harshly; as I tried to explain to her why we stopped payment on the back taxes--that my family was in a crisis-she told me she did not want to hear about my problems. She was only concerned about the information she wanted.

We did not let this incident break our spirit. We had faith, and when you have faith, you can move mountains or any obstacles that may get in your way. My wife continued her therapy, and we were still trying to get to the peak of her coordination. It had been so long since she walked that the muscles had to be redeveloped through many nights of therapy. She complained about stiffness and back aches, but all of this was about healing. I saw some improvements in her physical coordination. When transferring from the wheelchair to the car, I noticed that she got in and out of the car much easier.

For my wife's healing to take place, I had to psyche her up to over-come all obstacles, and not let her develop a mental block. I had to be strong mentally, physically, and emotionally.

There are some things in life that I will never understand. We say we live in a democratic society, but we are controlled by bourgeois, aristocratic, corporate giants who are sanguine for the rich, but asinine for the poor. These people have never been in the environment of the peasants. They never want to lower themselves to that standard. They have the power in America. They make the laws in Congress, and we poor have to live by their laws. These laws do not apply to them because the laws were made for the poor people.

The laws that are made for Internal Revenue were not voted on by me, but these ridiculous laws were made by lawyers who were elected into office. During the time my wife began improving her health, Internal Revenue threw a rotten apple in the basket that caused a retardation in her health progress once again.

I got a letter from Internal Revenue informing me that they were going to put a lien on my property. Well, at that time, my concern was my wife's health. I worked twenty-four hours a day trying to get her back to normal. I truly never rested. Sometimes I wondered what is holding me together. I know it had to be God. I did have my up and down periods, but I had no choice but to keep everything together. I called the lady at Internal Revenue to explain the situation about my wife's health. She did not want to hear what I had to say, just to answer the questions she wanted answered. I understood what she had to do, but someone needs to put professional people in that office to handle these cases, because they do not know how to talk to people. If I were someone with a heart condition, all they would do is help me to die by the way they talk to people. The Senate Finance Committee needs to do more than talk about it. They need to take immediate action; as we know from Internal Revenue there is no mercy. And no God, for Internal Revenue. What people fail to see is that the I.R.S. thinks it is God. It is only interested in your social security number and money, and that is all. For Internal Revenue, the constitutional citizenship and your Bill of Rights do not have any meaning. If it is not green, then it has no meaning.

I called the lady at the Internal Revenue Service and told her I would be sending her some information for 433, which is a collection information statement. They only have the information they want. There is nothing on there about one's health, because they did not tell me that I could file a 911 form or hardship. This is information that I read in their publication 594. It had the information that I needed to explain my wife's condition on the form; it only had eight lines to explain the hardship. Because of the severity of her condition, I wrote a special six-page statement of her condition, explaining that on February 26, 1997, my wife was rushed to Baton Rouge General Hospital. She was non-responsive and non-verbal for about twenty-minutes. Later she had three grand mal seizures. It took five people to hold her down. I explained that she was awoke the next day in ICU, not remembering anything. The doctors ordered an M.R.I. They placed her into a large cylinder or tube-shaped machine that took x-rays of her head and spinal area. She had blood tests done. The Thematologists, who treat all kinds of arthritis ailments, indicated she had Lupus; but she had been taken off steroids for five months. The Lupus got out of control, and she had alopecia.

Lupus is an auto immune disease where the white blood cells get confused and attack the good cells in the body and organs. The doctor immediately put my wife on a large dosage of steroids called prednisone, sixty milligrams everyday by mouth. During this time, they ran several tests. One showed she had spinal meningitis and another unknown virus. On the left front area of her head, there was something that was not a tumor or cancer, but it was unknown to the doctors. It was caused by alopecia diabetes. She stayed in the hospital for two weeks. After going home, she had to have physical therapy and was unable to walk. As she began to get physically better and wanted to go back to work at least two days a week, she found out her job had been filled. I tried to explain everything on the 911 form.

This is what I wrote on the six-page letter:

> "On May 22, 1997, our twenty-sixth wedding anniversary, my wife was awoken and was unable to move her legs or feel them. She

was put back into the hospital and found out she had a C.V.A. which is a stroke on the spinal cord. Her blood was too thick and caused the stroke, along with Lupus, which affected her nervous system. She remained in the hospital from May 22 until July 11, 1997. She had physical and occupational therapy to teach her how to get in and out of bed, into her wheelchair, on the bedside commode, and also how to take a shower. My wife's daily routine is to start the morning by taking the following pills," which I listed so the Internal Revenue Service could understand the seriousness of her condition. I wanted them to know what constituted my wife's daily routine. "She starts Prevacid, then Predinosone, Phenobarbital, Macrodatin, Bactrim, Zana Flex, Bacofen, Bisacodyl, Ultran, Macalgin, Neurontin, Dupaallac, Maalox, Advil, Novalin "N" insulin, Novalin "R" insulin, and Lachydrin."

I explained all this to the Internal Revenue Service so they could gain some understanding as to what was going on in my wife's daily life.

In this statement of conditions, I explained my daily tasks for my wife's as to her paralysis and what my responsibility was in giving her insulin shots in the morning, cleaning her, and placing a diaper on her. I am also responsible for catheterization, because she has no use of muscles that control her bladder. This occurs twice a day, also twice a week suppositories must be injected to take care of secretions.

I wanted Internal Revenue to get a clear understanding of our daily schedule and how everything is done in a time sequence.

In this statement of condition, I explained what happened and the reasons why we did not respond any sooner. Each day I was watching every mood and every sign of my wife, because she came so close to death earlier. We were doing really well until this dilemma was fabricated that put my family into total financial disaster. I explained the financial arrangements that caused my family not to function. The penalties and interests caused another thing to happen. We could not meet our financial needs in order to survive. Then I concluded with a written statement of all bills that we paid each month and all the medicine we had to purchase each month.

About a week later my wife received a phone call from a gentleman from Atlanta, explaining what we were to do and what the 911 Hardship Form would do. The gentleman was really nice; however, he explained that the lien against my retirement was lifted and told my wife that this payment did not release us of further payments, but it will always be there. I know that the people in the Internal Revenue Office did not know what the 911 meant. Another lady told me once I filed a 911 form, according to my wife's condition, they would have to throw it out. Now I understand. All this does is put a stop on payments, penalties, and interests, but it will always be there, and I will take this to my grave.

I just wonder sometimes, "What if I were born a foreigner and came to this country?" I know things for me would be so much better. In a way, I am glad this happened so this country can see the truth about being black in America. However, I do not want to use race as an issue because I know some whites are going through the same thing.

I hope that one morning I wake up to clear air a fragrance of sweet smells, a world of friendliness, without all the fears of nuclear war, Saddam Hussein, and Internal Revenue. I also hope I can wake up one morning when the government has more concern toward its citizens, and less about tax money.

I would love to wake up one morning with my wife back to normal, so she could go on and live a normal life. I would like to wake up one morning and find my wife in church by my side.

My wife was making tremendous progress in her therapy; then we got a letter in the mail announcing that the corporation was switching insurance. Some of the doctors who were treating here would have to be changed, because they have their own list of doctors and hospitals. The Baton Rouge General Hospital, where she received her treatment, was not on the list for her therapy. Just when she was getting her legs and body conditioned, she had to stop her therapy. This had a strong bearing on her healing-like an athlete, you cannot miss practice. Once you get the tone, you have to continue developing it.

I sat down, had a talk with my wife, psyched her up, and got her motivated again. We went to my brother-in-law's house on the weekend. She enjoyed it out there because you can have peace of mind, enjoy the smell of the honey suckle vine, take a deep breath, and send some fresh air to the brain. It is so quiet and peaceful, your mind will run away with you. Now I know why so many writers go on the outskirts of town to write, because they can concentrate in that kind of environment.

On Sunday morning as we drove up to my brother-in-law's drive-way, we noticed a walker was standing in the driveway. My brother-in-law's cousin remembered my wife needed this walker, so he went out his way to get the walker for her. When we drove up, I could see a glow in her eyes. She was very happy to see how someone was trying to help her. She could not wait until we got home to try it out, even though she could not go very far. She started doing about three feet, and she would practice standing up and sitting down. The next day she went about five feet, then the next day about fifteen feet.

Then she got a phone call telling her she could no longer take therapy at the Baton Rouge General any more, because Oschner would not permit it. So, I tried to get her some positive thoughts to help aid her motivation. I told her that we cannot change the system, but we can beat it! All we have to do is think of ourselves as a number one.

I told her if we cannot change the system, we can do our therapy at home. She had done five feet, then fifteen, and I also noticed she was taking longer strides that told me her legs were getting stronger. As she would walk, her legs would get weak; but soon she did thirty feet. In just a matter of time she could be walking freely or, shall I say, walking more like herself.

I said, "Go, Girl! It is just a matter of time, and you will be walking on the wild side!" Each time something bad happened, I would tell her she had to pick herself up again, because when you are going for the gold, you never give up, no matter what!

No one will ever know how hard it is when one is sick. I remember there were medicines she had to have, and there was a mix-up between the pharmacy and the doctor. My wife called the prescription in, but the pharmacy said the doctor's nurse had called it in. So, my wife called the doctor and she said the pharmacy had never called. All the time, my wife's life was on the edge. If she did not get the medicine, she could have a seizure. The last one caused her paralysis; the next one could cause her death. Even though she had so many odds against her, she still wanted to live. No one can ever know what it takes to survive this life, until it happens to you.

What I learned from all of this is that no matter what happens, you never give up. You have to always think positive. When things do not work for you, you have to fight the system.

I have a friend from Trinidad who is now an American. He said he did not understand the Americans. "How can they treat their citizens the way they treat me and my family?" he asked. "The American government can give millions of dollars to other countries, and at the same time treat their citizens like trash. They take their homes, belongings, and bank accounts and at the same time, when foreigners come to this country, the government gives them assistance," he said. He said he just did not understand the American government.

Your dreams, goals, health, religion, family, home, business, and Bill of Rights are just one gigantic explosion that shatters everything, caused by a branch of government-or is it a branch of government? I would think it operates as a separate entity with it's own Bill of Rights and Constitution; when one interferes, he or she gets audited automatically. Is the entity getting out of hand? Is what happened in Waco an example of the changes in government, the citizens becoming more rebellious, or is it a generation that is more rebellious? What is happening in the United States is a wake-up call. If something is not done soon, it could cause a catastrophe for our government. Why? Because generations are different, with different principles and different schooling. This generation is from the computer age and is much smarter.

What I would love to see happen to the next generation is government trying to prevent welfare, but at the same time, the government is also creating it. When this happens, there is something wrong with the system. This entity caused a catastrophe for my family. It caused pain and suffering. When something bothers someone, and it is constantly on their mind, and when this interferes with their religion, then it is infringing upon your Bill of Rights.

This entity caused the illness of my wife. It really affected her more than it affected me, because I had been conditioned for all situations. When you are prepared for war, you can handle any situation.

Who knows about the human body? It is the chemical makeup inside that causes change and variation in one's health-chemicals can cause a change in personality and cause illness. Hospitals are now having a psychiatrist analyze the patients, because they know that for healing to take place, the mind has to be right.

Some things this entity caused were: life re-adjustment, pressure, neglect, negative attitudes, changes in family values, living in extreme danger, destruction of my American dream, and lower values of life in general.

When a system creates a dilemma in a family that causes illness, hunger, and pain, then changes occur. I truly love being an American, but if I had political power, there are a lot of changes I would make. But I do not have that power and never will. One thing for sure, I would change the tax system that we have now. I would not allow the tax system to collect taxes on a person who is on disability with a serious ill-ness; I would definitely change the penalty and interest procedure in accordance to personal financial status. Also, I definitely would not allow the tax system to take someone's home. This is infringing on a citizen's Bill of Rights, the right to own a home. Th avoid embarrassment for my auditors, I would not allow them to advise a person with false information, and I would be sure all persons coming in for an audit were treated fairly.

Life is a dream. You wake up one morning and cannot remember how you got here or why you were put here. But you enjoy every part of the earth-wind, water, creative earth, mountains, trees, oceans, color combinations, rain, and the beautiful sunset with a rainbow. You know there is something magical about this. You were given an opportunity by God to live upon this wonderful earth. It was the intent of God for man to be free, equal, and have compassion for others-our sisters and brothers.

Man should not have to fear his own society and government. Man should allow him to negotiate or compromise. Would you believe it was an educated man who has twisted society with the rules and laws that even he does not live by?

In my sixty years of life, society has changed tremendously. You can see changes in society, from the ivy league look to hippie, from religious cult groups to militia groups. Now society is more camouflaged than back in the '50s. It really never came out of the closet. Something happened-it started with homosexuality, lesbianism, drug abuse, gangs, serial killering, pedophilia, and child abuse. Everything got out of hand. When man does not follow the commandments and rules of society, then things get out of control.

You wonder how those laws-made by educated people who have such a vast knowledge- get so twisted and complicated that even they cannot understand them. This is why our government is having so much trouble. It is because they are not going to the source. We act as though we are blind!

Now you know if we put man on the moon and put a craft on Mars, we can solve all of our problems on earth. We know that the majority of crime is centered around drugs. It causes robberies, killings, rapes, prostitution, and drug addicts! We can stop this, but we have a blind society. The prisons are full of young, black men who come from poor families. The youth that are being arrested are not the ones who are responsible for bringing the drugs into this country. It has to be brought in by some-one with money. It has to be someone in an executive position who has money, and that excludes the black guys in prison. You know they are not going to put a prominent person in prison. They are the people in the higher offices who have other people running things for them, so that they may keep their names from being revealed. They have inside people working for them so they can know what is going on at all times.

I remember an executive one time who was caught; I am willing to bet he is back on the street. I wish I had all the answers, but I know that little grandmother in the country can no longer live without fear. Everyday I fear that someone is going to break in on her. The other day I was driving my car when I smelled something burning inside. I later realized that it was the car in front of me. They were smoking marijuana. The safety of everyone depends on their safe driving. You have often heard the metaphor that a cat has nine live. By being human, you must have eighteen lives; that is why they play Russian Roulette.

I value every second of my life, because life is too short. You have to treat life like a game.

You have to act as though you are a winner all the time.

I try to plan each day with a schedule. I utilize every second of it, like an artist when painting a picture. You outline your life, then you paint the picture just the way you want your life to be. Always remember, life is longer when you include God with it.

I watched the mailbox each day, waiting for the letters to come. Each time the doorbell rang, I thought two men in black suits would be there to confiscate my belongings and take me to jail, to separate me from my family. Each time the phone rang, I feared it was a call from the Internal Revenue Service. Isn't it wonderful to have your government care so much about you, to show so much concern? I surely hope when they do come confiscate everything, that they leave me some underwear; I really would not want to leave this world naked. I hope the good guys do not take my wife's wheelchair. It takes all of this for me to have my freedom back and my constitutional rights to leave my family homeless, sleeping on the ground. They probably will give me some food stamps and let me have the medicines to continue working on my wife's health. If this is what democracy is about, then so be it. You know an old dog can be kicked around for so long, then one day he gets tired of it and bites you.

Is this why the Oklahoma bombing occurred? Is this why we have militia groups forming across the country? You do not have all the answers for God's children. Now I know what is meant by the expression, "Man will eventually destroy himself."

I guess you are saying I sound idiotic. Try walking in my shoes for a brief moment, and you will understand. I thought it very interesting that the Senate Finance Committee was investigating the wrongdoings of the Internal Revenue Service. They have the right idea about making changes; but there is one thing they did not mention. If you have a bushel of apples and a couple of apples are rotten, then to make changes you have to get rid of the rotten apples. So, what is needed to get rid of the inferior, rotten auditors and supervisors who created these dilemmas? I think they need to set up a symposium to discuss changes in the training program or require extensive training in psychology to learn how to talk to people. They need years of experience to learn the tax codes, so when the time arises, they will know what they are talking about and not give someone the wrong information. They need training in math to learn about business affairs and how businesses operate. The mistakes auditors make can affect citizens for life-just a mistake they make with a pen.

The University should offer a curriculum directly related to taxation, or offer degrees for auditors and master degrees for supervisors in higher offices. Once this is done, they should clean house and get rid of the bad apples. The government needs to come up with a flat tax; then they will be on their way to a good start. They should require everyone to pay taxes. Everybody will feel more safe in this country and not fear the month of April.

I remember when the Senate Finance Committee was investigating the I.R.S., the personality of the auditors I talked to never changed. The ones I talked to went on with business as usual, because they know that they are in charge of the government, and the government is not in charge of them. So, this is why we know if there are any changes to be made, we can put it back to the normal routine. The committee was just giving the public what they wanted to hear just to relax them; then months later, it will be forgotten-no changes will occur. We will have another president, other committee members, and we will continue doing what we have been doing- denying rights, collecting taxes, bringing in more foreigners and deferring their tax payment, and hassling Americans to pay their taxes. Then America will send more money to other countries to help house foreigners and worry about America's homeless later.

Now getting back to my family, the improvement of my wife continues. I had to psyche my wife up and tell her that good things are happening to us now. We have to close it out of our minds and act as though we are newborn, just entering this world. We have to start crawling all over. I told her there are four important things in life: God, conscious, common sense, and class. With all of these, we can make it. One thing I can say, I know that my wife has a strong spiritual connection with God. In all of my times I have never seen a person with such a high spiritual bond with God. I have seen God work miracles with her life. I have seen her pray for things, and when she finished, she would have that certain glow in her eyes that says, "It is done."

She prayed for my son-in-law to get a certain job, and a month later it happened. I have heard her say that God will heal her body, and she will walk again. She would say it with a smile; and I would have a solemn feeling in me that I, too, know that God's spiritual powers are very strong in this house. There is a supernatural thing happening in this house that I have never seen, and it has so much power. Just like her neurologist said, to be around her, you know that something is going on that is coming from another source.

As stated earlier, my wife had this stroke on the day of our anniversary. On that same day, she received a letter in the mall with a disability insurance check for an enormous amount. She had prayed to God that it would come through. After she received the letter she sat down, read the letter, and started crying. I did not know what was going on, so I asked her what was wrong. She said she prayed to God to send her the money for her disability, and it was answered.

One thing I have learned to do, in all of this, is to maintain control of my life. All the years of my life, all the love I have for all races-all the races are beautiful in their own way. I guess I just have a weak heart when it comes to people. When the Oklahoma bombing occurred, I cried for both black and white. When Thurston High School had that shooting, I felt like those people and I were related. I shared the feeling with the families; and when "Blue Eyes" died, there was a part of me that was taken away from my life. So I can say that many people that came and helped my family gave something back to me that the government had taken away. When something like this happens, and you know deep in your heart that you did not do anything wrong, then it really hurts. It has been really difficult writing this, because many times I had to stop, and cry, and try to regain my composure. There are times when I think about what happened to me-did that person have pre- conceived prejudices that resulted in my loss and her gain? I no longer feel like a citizen. All those years I thought I was a good citizen who exercised my rights and stood up for them, and I saw one person with the stroke of a pen destroy my life within a second. When the judge ordered my store closed, took my keys, and put a certain lady in charge as the trustee, she took over everything I owned. She went in and had equipment auctioned off for which I never saw papers showing what the items were sold for. I found out later that she had a moving company remove the remainder of the items. One day, while talking to an attorney, I found out she was no longer a trustee because she was using her company to move items while she was a trustee. Not one time did they come back and say they had to redo our case because of wrongdoings.

This is why I said I was cheated when I told the auditors that I had receipts showing I was putting personal money into the business. She refused to do anything to help me. When the Internal Revenue decided to audit me, the interest they applied was tremendous. If I take any longer, I can build it to the amount I want to and know how much money they make per year. I can fix it so that I can destroy them. I have all the powers, and I have all the penalties. When I get through with them, they will not be able to ever get caught up. I can destroy them because I have the power to do anything I want to. With my power, I can operate on this earth. I am God, and no one can stop me.

In the South, I found it strange that many of my black friends in business had the same thing happen to them. Was this a coincidence, or is there something going on that the public cannot, see? This is why I feel that I have cheated and betrayed; I do not have the American spirit. I do not celebrate any holidays or believe in the "red, white, and blue." All my life, it has been red when I see a foreigner in this country; I see that person as a citizen and not me.

I no longer celebrate Veteran's Day. My American spirit has been totally destroyed. I have seen the invasion of my civil rights, which I no longer have. I do not own any part of this country anymore. I, however, have no prejudice toward anyone because God does not want me to be that way. I have thought all my life that people were fair, but the experiences that my family and I went through that were brought on by these separate entities, that was not American. It was worse than my father's funeral. I really hope that no other family will have to go through what my family and I have gone through. I do not worry anymore, because God has power over all things.

You can play the games now, enjoy the prosperity of stealing from others, but in the end, all that you have accumulated-the marble tubs, big house, and BMW-was gained in an unjust fashion. At the end of your life, all the dirt you did to people will come to you in the end. The government business continues, but every person has a conscious and a soul. You will account for what you do in this life. I forgive you; but will you forgive yourself?

After all the things my wife and I have gone through, we realize that the only thing that is important in life is one's health, and everything else comes after that. Like a track star racing, you have many hurdles to jump over to get to the finish line. Well, it is never easy when you are running into many problems.

My wife was in therapy, learning how to walk again, when we received a letter from the insurance company informing us that the corporations had switched to another insurance company. Later we learned that this was not a good insurance company. Then we received information in the mail about what coverage we had and what doctors and therapists we could use; my wife had a setback. She was at a hospital, and it's therapy department was making tremendous progress; then the new insurance company would not accept that hospital because it was not on it's list. So, my wife's therapy stopped; she had to change all her doctors and could not use the ones she had been using because they were not on the insurance company's list. All the prescribed medicine had to get referred. The drugstore where the prescriptions were filled was having trouble with them going through the computer; we had to pay the full amount for the medicine. My wife had to call the insurance company and get an approval. Then we found out that the old insurance company had paid for everything. This new company would not pay for brand names and paid only a portion for generic brands. This company had to be the worst insurance company we had ever had. This put my wife in a state of depression once again. Finally, after so many hurdles, she got back on track again. Later she found out this company would only pay for a certain amount of therapy, so I decided to continue her therapy process. I would work with her each day, and I would help her to walk again. By July fourth, she had made amazing progress. I could see her legs getting stronger. I never realized that when a person has a stroke, it is like starting all over-like a child learning how to walk again. It has to be taken one step at a time.

While all this was going on, we had letters coming in the mail from different tax offices.

One in Washington advised us that we had a tax lien against us. We had filed a 911 form, which is a hardship form; you would think they would honor that form, but every other day we would receive a letter from other tax lawyers, commercializing and trying to a make a profit on our misfortune. One company sent me three letters telling me to come in for a free consultation. After my wife's therapy, we made an appointment with a lawyer. The lawyer wrote down all the information about our tax condition, informing me that the Internal Revenue Service could garnish my retirement check, and seize our bank accounts, motor vehicles, and life insurance. Then he asked me if I had any money. If I did not, I could offer Internal Revenue a compromise. He said Internal Revenue would accept fifteen cents for every dollar we owed. But my concern was what one auditor told me, that they could not collect the disability money. They would have to throw it out, or that money was uncollectible. But from what the lawyer said, they could collect the dis-ability money. I did not know what to believe. It seems as though no one really knew the answer; so who could I believe? The lawyer advised me about all the Internal Revenue matters; he said that for a fee of one hundred and sixty dollars an hour he could resolve this matter for me. But they also said I had to come up with a thousand-dollar retainer fee, plus what they charge per hour. So as you can see, it was all about money. Also, you see, when you are down, it seems like everyone wants a piece of the action.

I had to keep my wife in the right state of mind. We placed our focus on trying to go through the healing process. On the evening of July fifth, we concentrated on letting my wife walk on the floor for the first time. She did very well; that day she surprised me and walked from one room to the kitchen-about twenty-five feet-and she was really happy. For her reward, I gave her an ice cream sandwich to help motivate her. This was a good day for her. The next day I got up and went outside to feed the birds and came back inside; she was awake and ready for me to fix her breakfast. She was in high spirits that morning. She was ready to go and see her new doctor, but when we got there, the records had not been transferred to the office. She began to go into a negative state of mind. By this time, a friend walked into the doctor's office, and I spoke to him. "How are you?" I asked.

He did not hear me; his wife looked around and spoke. We had to fill out the paperwork that is required when you attend a new physician. My friend suddenly realized it was me, his old working buddy. He asked me how retirement was, and I told him that I had not eaten a meal since I left the plant. He started laughing.

By this time, the nurse came out to bring my wife into the doctor's office. My friend wanted to know how life had been, and I told him, "About the same." However, I told him what had happened to my wife-about her stroke-but he said she looked well. I added that she had made tremendous improvement. I explained to him about what God did for her, and he said his grandchild had something similar happen.

He said there was a medical problem internally, and the hospital in Baton Rouge could not find the problem. They found themselves going from one doctor to another. Finally, they got together with the doctors at Tulane Medical Center. They noticed the baby had lost an excessive amount of weight. The daughter decided they were going to a healing service that night; so the daughter decided she would ask the doctor if they could buy a little time. They were going to take the child to a prayer meeting; they did, and the child was healed. He said, "If you could see the baby today, you would say it was a miracle that happened."

I told him that experiencing something like this changes your whole life. Your attitude and personality will change your spiritual attitude and personal appearance. People who have had this experience are happy most of the time. They meet you with a smile. They have a jovial look. Like I said, miracles are all around us. We cannot recognize them all the time; physicians and nurses experience this all the time.

I recall a nurse telling me about her brother, who told her about his near-death experience. She said her mother died because she had a cerebellum hemorrhage. Her brother was having some chest congestions, so he went to the doctor. He told him they were going to rush him to the hospital. He said all he wanted was some medicine.

Then the doc-tor told him, "This is serious." They rushed him to the Veteran's Hospital. The nurse found her brother hooked up to IV's, and breathing machines, and all other types of medical equipment. The doctors at Veteran's Hospital found both lungs were full of congestion. They found he had double pneumonia. He was hooked up to life support machines.

He said that while all of this was going on he, too, noticed he was entering into darkness. Then as he approached the light, he was met by a host of other people. He said it was like a party; there were plenty of bright lights and food to eat. He said he told someone standing next to him that he felt like drinking a Coke because he was feeling so much better. The lady standing next to him told him he could not have a Coke. As he was leaving, the lady said, "You cannot have this Coke because you are going to continue to feel good. So he left the light but as he was leaving, he looked around. The lady that told him he could not have the Coke told him he had more important things to do with his life. He looked into her face, and the lady was his mother. The next morning when the nurses came, he was feeling better. He had disconnected the life support machine. He was breathing freely and was later released from the hospital. What I have noticed is that each person who tells about their his or her near-death experience, experiences a light. Each one has a different type of situation, and it is always some family member who is seen.

After coming from the doctor, my wife and daughter had a confrontation, and so my wife got a negative attitude. I remembered what I was taught in school about motivation, especially when a person is pessimistic. I already know the power of social support from your family and how to turn negative forces into positive forces. I started thinking about what I had to do that morning. I told her something to prevent her from developing anxiety; I took a negative force and turned it into a positive force. I told my wife that we were going to have therapy this morning, and she started walking to the kitchen and back to the bedroom. When we measured the distance, she had walked fifty-five feet. My wife got really happy because she noticed she was not tired; but I did not want to press her because I did not want to cause any regression. We continued where we left off the next day, and we turned a negative force into a positive force. She noticed that life can change in a few seconds. It depends on your attitude, because emotions can affect you physically. For healing to take place, you must have the love of your family. One thing about spiritual guidance is that one should not let the problem be isolated or leave it in the closet. When we discuss our problem and keep it in an optimistic form, then this gives medicine to the person who has the illness.

Whenever you are sick, the mind will play tricks with you. I recall when my wife had a sort of scary moment; she was standing and went into a trance. She could hear the therapist talking to her, but she got dizzy and thought she was going to have a seizure. The human body is difficult to understand. I told her she could have been experiencing something brought on by her medication, or maybe she got too hot, but not to worry about it because it the seizure did not happen. Think positive, and only put good memories into your mind so that healing continues.

I have to be observant at all times. I noticed that when we were riding in the car, she would never sit back on the seat of the car. I asked her why. She told me that she can feel pain in her back with each pot hole I hit in the street, so I have to be really careful about my driving.

A long time ago, when my wife was diagnosed with Lupus, I told her I had a feeling that somewhere in the world, someone was going to come with medicine that will cure Lupus. While I was watching television, they announced that they have a cure for Lupus. My heart started to beat really fast. I was excited because this was a dream come true for anyone with Lupus. I immediately got a pen. They announced the address to write for more information on how it was done and the result of the research. They explained the different types of Lupus. Lupus is a rheumatic disease that affects the joints and muscles. Lupus also can affect the immune system. Lupus can affect the kidneys, nervous system, lungs, and blood. I was watching the news on Channel Two when it was announced. It gave me hope for my wife, because I have seen how devastating this disease is and what it can do to a person. It makes one's life miserable, and all this happens in a split second. When this was announced, I wanted to kiss the people who were responsible for such a great discovery. I personally wanted to thank the UCLA

Medical Center, the Fred Hutchinson Cancer Research Center, and Dr. Richard Burt. These individuals deserve awards, because they care about people. My personal thanks goes out to them for relieving my mind and my wife's mind and giving us hope that there is a chance at life even when you have Lupus. This hematopoietic cell transplant will help many Lupus patients, and give them back their lives.

Even though my wife's Lupus is in remission, it is good to know there is life after Lupus. The next day, we awoke to a brighter day, with less fear, and that morning we had the spirit as we went to therapy. I pushed my wife in, and we spoke to everybody. We said good morning, and no one parted his or her lips. I went in, signed the register, and smiled at the people and acted as though nothing had happened. I proceeded to talk to my wife about a catalog in which we were getting ready to order some collectibles. Time went by fast.

By this time, a white lady with her son and daughter walked in. Her son went to sit in the corner alone. The mother must have been having trouble with him. She told him to sit in the corner, and she did not want him running around the office. She went in for her therapy, and he sat there like a little gentleman. We must have sat there for about forty-five minutes; a white friend of mine walked up and shook my hand. By this time, my wife came out; my friend went on to sign the register, and my wife went to the door. There was a white gentleman sitting by the door in a wheelchair. While I was grabbing my books to get up to help her, my wife had already made it to the door. As she got to the door, the white gentleman ignored her while she was trying to open the door. The young white gentleman got up and held the door open for my wife. I was shocked because seeing the younger generation being so helpful is rare these days. My wife thanked him, and I thanked him and told him he was a real gentleman, because he did it from the heart. Because of my wife's condition, the younger gentleman wanted to do something very special for her. As for his mother, after giving her a hard time, he probably made her day when he told her about the very special thing he did. After thanking him, I asked him if I could buy him a Coke, and he said, "Yes." Instead, I gave him a dollar, because I saw something special in him. What I saw in him was maturity and culture; more than that, he wanted to be a gentleman. His mother worried about him being good, but what she did not know was that she should look from the sideline and discover a new son. What he did for my wife added healing to her every time she would think about him. It truly makes me feel good about the races. He also taught me something-that you cannot judge single incidents as an example for all. I think that in life we look for too much good; what we need to understand in life is that people do not feel good all the time. Why should we expect this when we do not feel good all the time ourselves?

My wife continued her therapy. I noticed tremendous improvement. She began standing on her own; some of the things we wanted, started occurring. I got up one morning, made some coffee, and got the newspaper. On the front page was an article on the overhaul of Internal Revenue. The senate announced the changes were as follows: creating a new post of treasury inspector general; setting up some safeguards to help protect taxpayers from unreasonable audits; and baring the building of interest for taxpayers filing late returns or extensions all together. There were about fifteen different provisions, but once again one of the main issues not mentioned was requiring auditors to have extensive training related to dealing with people, a psychology course, and a course in mathematics or business. They should require I.R.S. auditors to go to school and receive a degree in the field, just like any other curriculum.

At my wife's last therapy session, they told us the insurance would not pay for any more therapy. This insurance company has it's own rules; I guess they do not have any federal guidelines. I have never seen anything like this before in my life. That evening, I went to pick up her medicine, and the insurance company refused to pay for it. My wife and many other families are going through the same thing; this is what hap-pens when one is at the edge of life. It seems like no one cares anymore in that moment when we thought the drugstore was not going to fill her prescription for her steroid medicine. If she could not get it, it would cause her death from what was explained to me, but finally the pre-scription went through.

After her insurance stopped therapy, we decided we were not going to stop progress; I would administer the therapy. I planned to drill her like an army sergeant. Instead of having therapy two days a week, we would have it twice a day, every day. We started in the middle of the week. I had already noticed her legs getting stronger within just a few days. She began to stand better, and her spirit was high. I could forget my other troubles and concentrate on her motivation.

I feel really good about her in the mornings. I roll out of the bed early in the morning, prepare her breakfast, give her a shot, then we are ready for her day. In the morning, she looks forward to seeing her daughter go to school with her nurse's uniform on, holding her grandson. She looks at our grandson with the widest smile, and then he is off to school. My daughter is a remarkable lady. She had a baby while attending school and had problems with her boyfriend, but this never stopped her from going to school. She still make good grades; after all the misfortune we had, this is one thing the American government did that was good. They provided a loan for her to finish college. The time went really fast, and now she is graduating; this really makes me feel as though we accomplished something in life, although I feel I should march with her because we went through so much to get there.

After feeling like an outcast in society, I realize that it will always be this way until the die- hards pass away. This generation will change; blacks will no longer be ridiculed in American society. No longer will society stop it's description of studies comparing black and white health problems and who has the best health, and no longer will an application have race on it. The computer will be testing for employment and hiring; there will be a new tax system. The population in America will have so many foreigners that blacks and whites will be the minority. The medical profession will change; God will become the major part of healing in hospitals.

Because anti-American groups keep developing, the FBI will be like a small army in America. The nations around the world will no longer concentrate on modern nuclear weapons; they will be fighting for survival because of new weather conditions that will become a big enemy to mankind. Homes will become more compact, but more sophisticated; engineers will develop a small engine about the size of a motorcycle engine, and it will be seal-proof, with tremendous power.

Fire will no longer threaten the households. The homes will have a smoke detector that will have an extinguisher to automatically spray any fire where wires or hot water heaters are located. Any place where a spark can occur will have this new technology installed. This system will have a control center in homes and will let you know where the problems are located. Fashion will change completely because of global warming. I have already designed clothes for the future. I think this, too, has motivated my wife's health, because I made a prototype which I am in the process of getting patented. Every time she looks at it, she is fascinated by this invention. I took it out late one night to test the invention, and it was like going into another dimension. With all the problems we have had, God implanted innovation in my mind to distract me from the evil things that have been happening to us. One day, one of these innovations will go through and open up the avenues to my other inventions. In the last fifteen years, I have developed more than ten inventions in my home; everyday something new comes up because I see things differently than others. This has been my gift from God. Each time one invention develops, then something happens that stops me for completing it. Right now, my biggest challenge is the government and my wife's health, but what has happened to me in the past has changed me. I have become more guarded but a better person, because I incorporate God the leader in everything I do. This includes my inventions. For any task I have to challenge, or crisis I have to face, I develop a plan.

"The eternal God is thy refuge, and underneath are the everlasting arms; and He shall thrust out the enemy from before thee; and shall say, Destroy them." (Deuteronomy 33:27)

"I will lift up mine eyes unto the hills, from whence cometh my help. My help cometh from the Lord, which made heaven and earth. He will not suffer thy foot to be moved: He that keepeth thee will not slumber. Behold, He that keepth Israel shall neither slumber nor sleep. The Lord is thy keeper: the Lord is thy shade upon thy right hand. The sun shall not smite thee by day, nor the moon by night. The Lord shall pre-serve thee from all evil: He shall preserve thy soul. The Lord shall pre-serve thy going out and thy coming in from this time forth, and even for evermore." (Psalms 121:1-8)

Now when I have problems, there is only one person who can help me. I hide in a corner and shed my tears. When I am full of fear, and my wife has her problems so I cannot share my problems with her and I do not want to bother my eighty-five-year-old mother, I turn to God. I am a man, but weak, with friends who cannot be there all the time; so I turn to God and read John for comfort in troubling circumstances.

"These things I have spoken unto you, that in me ye might have peace. In the world ye shall have tribulation: But be of good cheer; I have overcome the world." (John 16:33)

"Paul, an Apostle of Jesus Christ by the will of God, and Timothy our Brother, unto the church of God which is at Corinth, with all the saints which are in all Achaia: Blessed be God, even the Father of our Lord Jesus Christ, the Father of mercies, and the God of all comfort; Who comforteth us in all our tribulation, that we may be able to comfort them which are in any trouble, by the comfort where with we ourselves are comforted of God. For our rejoicing is this, the testimony of our con-science, that in simplicity and Godly sincerity, not with fleshly wisdom, but by the grace of God, we have had our conversation in the world, and more abundantly to your ward. But we had the sentence of death in our-selves, that we should not trust in ourselves, but in God, which raiseth the dead." (11 Corinthians 1:1, 3, 4, 9, 12)

Now that we have reached the final phase of our lives, we realize there are some things in life that man cannot change-the evil eternity. I cannot change it, it will be there: taxes, penalties, and my wife's health. I asked my wife how she felt about it and how has this changed her. She said she has been through a traumatic experience. This was the hardest thing she has ever had to do. She wanted to live. She found out who God was and what He could do. This made it easier for her to live. She became a new person inside and outside. She is filled up inside with enough love to fill the world, an inner peace that she never knew existed. She sees everyone and everything as being beautiful and being so forgiving to all the sinful things. She can hardly wait to be at the right hand of her Father.

"Putting God first gives you all these wonderful things. Aren't you glad you are saved?" Those were her exact words. I am a different person. I no longer feel like an outcast. I realize that what I have on this earth is immaterial to me. What I want are the stars of the heavens, an angel, and to sit at the right hand of my God, my Father.

Verses taken from the *Holy Bible*, King James Version, Red Letter Edition, Regency Publisher.